A WALKER'S GUIDE
TO THE PUBS OF DARTMOOR

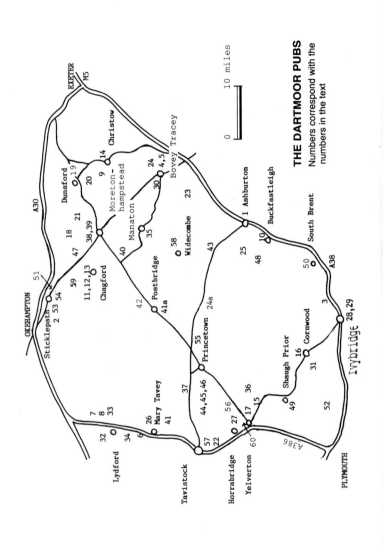

THE DARTMOOR PUBS

Numbers correspond with the numbers in the text

0 ─── 10 miles

A WALKER'S GUIDE TO
THE PUBS OF DARTMOOR

by

Chris Wilson & Michael Bennie

CICERONE PRESS
MILNTHORPE, CUMBRIA

ISBN 1 85284 115 X

British Library Cataloguing-in-Publication Data. A catalogue record for
this book is available from the British Library.

ACKNOWLEDGEMENTS

We would like to thank Kyle Taylor for his help in compiling this
guide, Jonathan Bennie for drawing the maps and taking the
photographs, and Brendan ("Jack") Russell for putting the idea into
our heads.

Advice to Readers

Readers are advised that whilst every effort is taken by the author
to ensure the accuracy of this guidebook, changes can occur
which may affect the contents. It is advisable to check locally on
transport, accommodation, shops etc but even rights-of-way can
be altered and, more especially overseas, paths can be eradicated
by landslip, forest fires or changes of ownership.

The publisher would welcome notes of any such changes

CONTENTS

The Oxenham Arms, South Zeal (see page 117)

INTRODUCTION

Why a *walker's* guide to pubs? Of course, many of us like to finish our walks with a drink or a meal, and some of us enjoy stopping off along the way. But what is wrong with the general pub guides already available?

The answer is nothing - if what you want is general information. But do they tell you whether the landlord objects to hikers tramping across his carpets in muddy boots? Do they say what walking there is in the vicinity, whether you can leave your car there overnight, or whether they offer bunkhouse accommodation? No they don't - that's not what they are for. So for the walker, finding a pub that has the facilities and atmosphere you want can be something of a hit-and-miss affair. We hope this *walker's* guide will help to make it less so.

One of the problems with many pub guides is that all too often you have to work your way through a maze of description to find the nugget of information you need. We have therefore deliberately kept the entries as simple as possible, while providing all the information you might want. The first part of each entry provides a quick, at-a-glance guide to the facilities the pub offers: the beers they have, car parking facilities, whether they do food, whether they have accommodation, whether they allow children and dogs, etc. This is followed by a more extensive description: the pub's atmosphere, the landlord's attitude to walkers, interesting features, as well as a few details of the local area, traditions and legends. We don't pretend that the descriptions are exhaustive - we have not described all the decorations and furnishings in every case. Instead we have tried to give a "feel" for the pub; sometimes this has involved giving a detailed description, at other times not. And of course, in a book of this kind the views and descriptions are inevitably our own personal reactions to the pubs when we have visited them.

The selection is also, of course, a personal matter. We have listed those pubs that we've found most congenial or convenient. Generally we have tried to restrict ourselves to one or two pubs per town or village, but in two towns - Chagford and Princetown - this has not been possible. They are major centres for both visitors and walkers, and the pubs we have listed - three in each town - all have their own characters, and are all worth a mention.

We have omitted one or two pubs that we would have liked to include because the publicans have specifically asked not to be listed and we have, of course, had to respect their wishes, however regretfully. Two pubs that are great favourites with walkers, the East Dart Hotel at Postbridge and the Forest Inn at Hexworthy, closed down while we were preparing this book, and were originally omitted. However, they have since re-opened and we have managed to add them in at the last minute. That is why they are numbered 41a and 24a respectively: they were included too late for us to change the whole numbering system to accommodate them, but they are really too important to be left out.

The listings are in alphabetical order by location, but there is an index of pub names at the end of the book if you are looking for a specific pub.

A few words about letter-boxing may not go amiss here. Letter-boxing is a popular pastime with many locals and visitors. A Dartmoor letter box consists of a rubber stamp, usually in the form of a picture of some sort, and a pad, and they are scattered all over the moor, usually hidden under rocks, between the roots of trees or in caves and cracks. Letter-boxers walk from letter box to letter box "collecting" the stamps on their own pads or pieces of paper. Some individuals and groups even have their own stamps made, and leave a record of their visit in the letter box. Many pubs have cashed in on the popularity of this pastime by having their own stamps made for their customers to collect. We have therefore indicated for the benefit of existing or potential letter-boxers whether the pub has its own letter box stamp.

This is not a walking guide, but we have provided ideas for interesting walks around each pub, to give you a "flavour" of what's available. We suggest you use the Ordnance Survey Outdoor Leisure Map No.28 to plan your walks. But do remember the safety code - walking on the moors after too much alcohol is dangerous. Remember too that Dartmoor is a fragile environment. If we treat it with respect, we will be able to enjoy it for many generations to come. If we don't, we will destroy it and deny ourselves and our children the pleasures it affords.

We have deliberately interpreted the term "Dartmoor" fairly loosely. You will find places here that are not strictly within the boundaries of the National Park, but which are regarded by most locals as being part of Dartmoor. We have generally used the main roads, particularly the A30 in the north and the A38 in the south, as our limits, rather that the National Park boundaries themselves.

Finally, an invitation. If you have a favourite pub we haven't mentioned, if there are any features we haven't covered or if you would like to give your own views on any of the pubs listed, we would be delighted to hear from you, and your comments could be incorporated into future editions of the guide.

* * *

Ashburton

1. The Exeter Inn

Map Reference:	755699
Open:	11.00-2.30, 5.30-11.00
Type:	Free house
On Draught:	Bass, Ruddles Best, Badger Best, Webster's, Guinness, Carlsberg Lager, Carlsberg Export, Inch's Cider
Children:	In the lounge
Dogs:	Yes
Food:	Midday and evening
Letter Box Stamp:	No
Parking:	No. There is a pay and display car park just behind the pub, down a side lane.
Accommodation:	No
Facilities:	Beer garden. Shove ha'penny, darts, dominoes, cards, backgammon.

Description:
There are, of course, several pubs in Ashburton, but this is our favourite. Despite the lack of parking, and its rather unpromising exterior, it is a delightful place. It is one of the oldest pubs in Devon, dating back to 1130, built to accommodate the workers who were building the church across the road. Sir Walter Raleigh was arrested here.

It consists of two rooms. There is a small, cosy bar at the front, with low beams and a stone fireplace with an open fire. Behind the bar is the mantelpiece of the original fireplace, a massive piece of stone that according to the landlady supports the whole pub! In days gone by, apparently, horses were brought in to be shod at that fire.

Beyond the bar is a snug, comfortable lounge, with stone walls, furnished with upholstered benches and chairs, and behind the pub a pretty little courtyard which is used as a beer garden.

This is very much a "local" with its regular clientele. It is a friendly, welcoming place with a very warm atmosphere.

Local Interest:
Ashburton is an old stannary town on the south-western edge of Dartmoor. Because it is within the National Park, development has been limited and it has retained much of its charm.

A few miles outside the town is the River Dart Country Park, a large area of wood- and parkland which incorporates a residential centre. There is an adventure playground, woodland walks, a bathing lake and a variety of other family attractions.

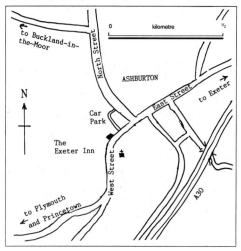

THE EXETER INN, ASHBURTON

Walks:
There are some pleasant walks - through lanes and farmland to Whiddon Wood in the north, and to the Dart and along the riverside in the west. There are one or two beautiful places to picnic on the river bank. In neither direction is the walking very taxing, nor is the terrain typical of Dartmoor, but they are delightful country rambles nevertheless.

Belstone

2. The Tors Inn

Map Reference:	620936
Open:	11.00-2.30, 6.30-11.00
Type:	Free house
On Draught:	Dartmoor Strong, Butcombe Bitter, Cockleroaster Winter Warmer, Newquay Steam Bitter, Ansells, Murphy's Stout, Carlsberg Lager, Carlsberg Export, Inch's Stonehouse Cider
Children:	Yes
Dogs:	On a lead
Food:	Midday and evening
Letter Box Stamp:	Yes
Parking:	In the village
Accommodation:	3 rooms
Facilities:	Dining room. Darts. Pub sweatshirts available at the bar.

Description:
This stone-built pub dates back about 100 years and has something of a "turn-of-the-century" appearance, with a high ceiling and high windows. It is a long, narrow building, with one rather Spartan-looking bar furnished with tables and chairs and with a wood-

burning stove at the end. There is an interesting collection of beer mats above the bar. The dining room is at the far end of the building, past the toilets and kitchen, and is a pleasant, rather cosy room, with high-backed settles to sit on. Walkers are made very welcome.

Food:
The food ranges from sandwiches and ploughman's lunches to main meals, and there is an interesting selection of specials on the board.

Local Interest:
Belstone is a pretty little village just south of the A30 near Okehampton. This is Tarka the Otter country, with the River Taw running past the village. There is also pony trekking nearby.

Walks:
There is a lovely walk along the river to Sticklepath, or you can leave the river at Skaigh and explore Skaigh Wood. To the south lies the open moor, with Belstone Common just to the south and Cawsand

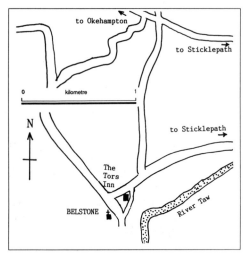

THE TORS INN, BELSTONE

Beacon (marked Cosdon Beacon on the OS map) to the south-east. This is wild country and should be treated with caution in bad weather. Check on firing times before venturing too far, as this is a military range.

Bittaford

3. The Horse and Groom

Map Reference:	667569
Open:	11.00-3.00, 5.30-11.00
Type:	Ushers house
On Draught:	Courage Best, Ushers Best, John Courage Strong, Beamish Stout, Fosters Lager, Kronenbourg Lager, Strongbow Cider
Children:	At the two ends of the bar
Dogs:	On a lead
Food:	Midday and evening
Letter Box Stamp:	5 stamps
Parking:	Yes. Ask about overnight parking.
Accommodation:	3 rooms
Facilities:	Darts, euchre, dominoes

Description:

The present pub was built at the turn of the century, to replace the original inn, of the same name, which was across the road. It comprises a long, straight bar, with seating areas at each end, and a beautiful open log fire in the middle.

It is a very pleasant pub, nicely carpeted and furnished with upholstered benches and tables. It is decorated with several interesting old photographs of the local area.

Food:
The menu ranges from bar snacks to full meals, soups to sweets, steaks to vegetarian dishes.

Local Interest:
Bittaford is a rather sprawling village right on the southern edge of the National Park. Wrangaton Golf Course is nearby, and there is pony trekking in the area.

Walks:
There are several walks to the north of Bittaford, and Western Beacon is about a mile (1.5km) (and a fairly steep climb!) to the north-east. Beyond Western Beacon you can join the Two Moors Way, and follow it as far north as you like.

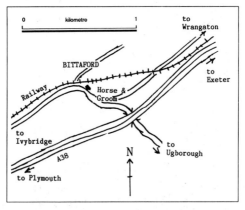

THE HORSE AND GROOM, BITTAFORD

Bovey Tracey

4. The Old Thatched Inn

Map Reference: 813781
Open: 11.00-3.30, 5.30-11.00

The Bearslake Inn, near Bridestowe

The Angler's Rest, Fingle Bridge

The Church House Inn, Holne

The Forest Inn, Hexworthy

Type:	Free house
On Draught:	Pedigree, Wadworth 6X, Royal Wessex, West Country PA, Whitbread Best, Newquay Steam Bitter, Newquay Steam Pils, Murphy's Stout, Guinness, Heineken Lager, Scrumpy Jack Cider
Children:	Yes
Dogs:	Yes
Food:	Midday and evening (flambé menu evenings only)
Letter Box Stamp:	Yes
Parking:	Free public car park next door
Accommodation:	No
Facilities:	Dining room. Beer garden. Pool, darts. Disco every second Tuesday.

Description:

A seventeenth-century coaching inn, very well preserved and decorated. There is just the one, long bar, almost divided in two by the large chimney in the middle. There are fireplaces on both sides of the chimney. The bar is at one end of the room and the pool table and darts board at the other. There is a stone floor and low oak beams, and the bar is furnished with upholstered settles and wheel-back chairs. The dining room is carpeted and nicely furnished, and there is a pleasant beer garden.

Walkers are made very welcome, and of course with its stone floor, there is no problem with wet and muddy gear.

Food:

There is a wide range of bar snacks (including seven kinds of jacket potato) and main meals, as well as daily specials. The speciality is their flambé menu, which is on offer five days a week, evenings only.

Local Interest:

Bovey Tracey is a pleasant little town just to the east of the National Park. Although it is not actually within the Park boundary, the

National Park Authority's headquarters are here, and it is to all intents and purposes part of Dartmoor. Within the town is the showroom of the Devon Guild of Craftsmen, with many local crafts on display, and items for sale. At Parke, on the outskirts, where the Park Authority's headquarters are, there is also an interesting rare breeds farm, which is worth a visit. There is fishing on the River Bovey.

Walks:
You can walk from Bovey to Parke, join the disused railway line and do an undemanding and beautiful circular walk of the Parke Estate, most of it on National Trust land. Beyond Parke, there is a variety of walks in Houndtor Wood, on Trendlebere Down or around Haytor. Just within the Park boundary lies Yarner Wood, a National Nature Reserve, with some lovely woodland trails.

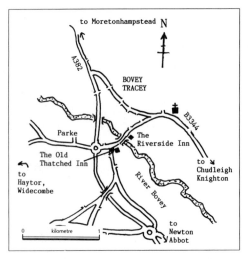

THE OLD THATCHED INN AND THE RIVERSIDE INN, BOVEY TRACEY

The Riverside Inn, Bovey Tracey

5. The Riverside Inn

Map Reference:	816783
Open:	11.00-11.00
Type:	Free house
On Draught:	West Country PA, Pedigree, Bass, Whitbread Trophy, Stella Artois Lager, Heineken Lager, Dry Blackthorn Cider
Children:	Yes
Dogs:	On a lead
Food:	Midday and evening
Letter Box Stamp:	Yes
Parking:	Yes
Accommodation:	10 rooms, all with en suite bathrooms
Facilities:	Restaurant. Function room. Beer garden. Fishing on the river adjoining the pub.

Description:
Right by the river, this seventeenth-century inn has a large,

19

L-shaped bar, with little alcoves, which merges into the beautiful restaurant area. The food is served at a separate food bar near the restaurant area. The walls are mainly bare stone and there is a large open fire near the bar and some interesting carving above the bar itself. The room is thickly carpeted and furnished with upholstered settles and stools and "barrel" tables, and there is gentle piped music playing all the time, all of which gives a somewhat luxurious atmosphere.

Walkers needn't be overawed by the plushiness, however. The owners are themselves keen walkers, and happily welcome fellow enthusiasts.

Food:
There is a wide range of delicious home-made bar snacks, main meals and daily specials from the food bar, and an à la carte restaurant menu. Their speciality is the 3-course Sunday lunch.

Local Interest:
See previous entry.

Walks:
See previous entry.

Brentor

6. The Brentor Inn

Map Reference:	472810
Open:	11.00-2.30, 6.00-11.00 (summer) 7.00-11.00 (winter)
Type:	Free house
On Draught:	Bass, Flowers Original, Whitbread Best, Bentley's, Guinness, Newquay Steam XXX, Carlsberg Lager, Stella Artois Lager, Bulmers Original Cider
Children:	Yes, except in the bar

Dogs:	On a lead
Food:	Midday and evening
Letter Box Stamp:	Yes
Parking:	Yes. Ask about overnight parking.
Accommodation:	2 rooms
Facilities:	Restaurant. Family room. Conservatory. Games room with pool, darts and video games in summer. Beer garden.

Description:

This is an interesting inn, basically seventeenth-century but with a few more recent additions. One enters through one of these additions, the conservatory, a delightful room running the length of the pub, with ivy growing over the rafters, furnished with tables and wooden benches.

The bar is a very welcoming room with attractive slate walls and a stone floor, and a large open fire at one end. Beyond the fireplace is the small but comfortable restaurant. Off the bar is the small, cosy family room with a piano and tables and chairs, and right at the back of the pub is the games room, another recent addition, with two pool tables and a dart board. There are video games in summer. The beer garden is at the back.

The pub has one or two interesting features. To the right of the fireplace is a face in the stonework, which has been seen to change expression from time to time. And under one of the flagstones in front of the fire there is said to be a tunnel leading to the church of St Michael of the Rock on top of Brent Tor. Since no one has ventured to excavate it, the story cannot be proved. The pub is also said to be haunted by the ghost of Phil Herring, who lived in the locality some centuries ago.

Food:

There is a range of bar snacks and main meals, from jacket potatoes to steaks, as well as daily specials on the board.

Local Interest:

Brentor is a small village on the western edge of the National Park, about 2¹/₂ miles (4km) south-west of Lydford. The pub is not actually in the village itself, but further west, just below the tor, which is a popular place to visit because of the church on the top. Lydford Gorge, a very popular National Trust site, is a mile (1.5km) or so to the north-east.

Walks:
Apart from the climb up Brent Tor, there are walks to Mary Tavy, Gibbet Hill and Black Down to the east, with the open moor beyond the A386 (but check firing times if you are going onto the open moor here, as it is a military range). There is also a path leading to Lydford Gorge, and beautiful walks through the gorge itself.

THE BRENTOR INN, BRENTOR

nr Bridestowe

7. The Bearslake Inn

Map Reference:	529889
Open:	Summer: 11.00-3.00, 6.30-11.00 Winter: 12.00-2.30. 7.00-11.00
Type:	Free house
On Draught:	Dartmoor Best, Wadworth 6X, Falstaff Keg, Guinness, Castlemaine Lager
Children:	In the beer garden and restaurant only
Dogs:	No
Food:	Midday and evening
Letter Box Stamp:	No
Parking:	Yes
Accommodation:	6 rooms with en suite bathrooms. Dogs allowed in rooms. Caravan site for 6 caravans (Caravan Club registered).
Facilities:	Restaurant. Beer garden.

Description:
This is a beautiful old thirteenth-century Devon longhouse, which was once a working farm. It is thatched, with old stone walls and a stone floor, and looks very pretty from the outside. Unfortunately the effect is somewhat spoilt by a modern interior, which is out of character with the outside appearance, and a rather sterile atmosphere. There is just the one small bar. The staff are very welcoming and they offer special discounted weekend breaks for walkers during the winter months.

The place is said to be haunted by a young girl. She was apparently at a window watching her mother riding when she fell down the stairs and was killed.

Food:
There is a variety of bar snacks, including four different kinds of

23

ploughman's lunch. The restaurant offers both à la carte and table d'hôte menus. A speciality is their Sunday carvery.

Local Interests:
This inn is situated right on the A386 between Okehampton and Tavistock, on the extreme western edge of the moor. There is a direct access on to the moor via a bridle path which runs right past it, and there is pony trekking nearby.

Walks: This is open moorland, which means that there are few designated footpaths, but you can wander almost anywhere to the north, east or south. This area is a military range, so check on firing times before venturing too far. It is also wild and rough, so care should be taken, especially in bad weather.

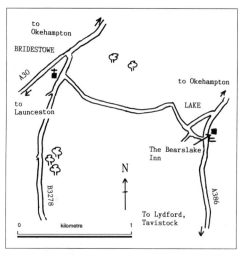

THE BEARSLAKE INN, nr BRIDESTOWE

8. The Fox and Hounds Hotel

Map Reference:	525866
Open:	11.00-11.00
Type:	Free house
On Draught:	Flowers IPA, Boddingtons, Pedigree, Whitbread Best, Guinness, Heineken Lager, Carlsberg Lager, Strongbow Cider
Children:	Under control
Dogs:	Yes
Food:	Midday and evening
Letter Box Stamp:	Yes
Parking:	Yes
Accommodation:	6 rooms, all with en suite bathrooms. 2 rooms in a separate cottage. Camping and caravan site. There are plans for a bunkhouse.
Facilities:	Games room with darts, pool, skittles, games machines. Beer garden with children's play area.

The Fox and Hounds Hotel, nr. Bridestowe

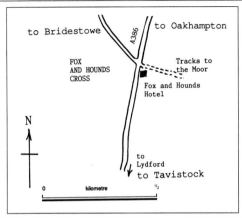

THE FOX AND HOUNDS HOTEL, nr. BRIDESTOWE

Description:
There has been a pub on this site for many years, although the present building only dates back to 1902. It is a large, family-run stone-built hotel with a friendly atmosphere and a warm welcome for visitors. There is a single bar divided into two, with an open fire in each section. The walls are partly of open stone, partly panelled and partly papered. There is an interesting painting on one of them which was done by a German prisoner of war.

Walkers are made extremely welcome - there is even a special accommodation rate for them. There are plans to build a barbecue area for the use of campers and other residents.

Food:
There is a variety of bar snacks, ranging from sandwiches to steaks and vegetarian specialities, as well as an à la carte restaurant menu. The food is home cooked, and fresh vegetables are used wherever possible. There is a special traditional roast beef dinner on Sundays. Breakfast is served to all comers from 9 to 11 o'clock.

Local Interest:
The hotel is situated on the A386 between Tavistock and Okehampton, south-east of Bridestowe and just on the western edge of Dartmoor.

26

Walks:
A track leads eastwards on to the moor, and from there the possibilities are almost endless. This is open moorland, and you can walk almost anywhere to the north, south or east. The nearest tors are Arms Tor and Little Links Tor, but there are many more waiting to be explored further afield. Remember that this is a military range, so check on firing times before venturing too far. It is also rough and wild, so take care, especially in bad weather.

Bridford

9. The Bridford Inn

Map Reference:	816865
Open:	12.00-2.30, 7.00-11.00 (6.30-11.00 in summer). Closed Tuesdays
Type:	Free house
On Draught:	Palmers IPA, Bass, Dartmoor Strong, Flowers Best, Guinness, Carlsberg Lager, Warsteiner Lager, Addlestone's Cider (Guest beer each week)
Children:	In the family annexe
Dogs:	Yes
Food:	Midday and evening (closed Tuesdays)
Letter Box Stamp:	No
Parking:	Yes. Ask about overnight parking.
Accommodation:	No
Facilities:	Small function room. Family annexe. Beer garden. Pool table.

Description:
This pub has only been in existence about 25 years. It was originally a row of seventeenth-century cottages, but has been extremely tastefully converted. There is one large bar with the small family

27

The Bridford Inn, Bridford

annexe off it. It still has the original bare stone walls in parts, and there are low beams and a large stone fireplace with comfortable armchairs on either side.

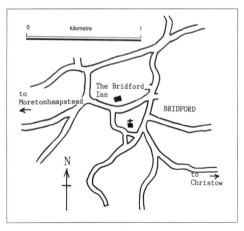

THE BRIDFORD INN, BRIDFORD

The rest of the bar is furnished with tables, settles and wheel-back chairs and the floor is carpeted. The bar itself is interesting - it is considerably wider than most bars, because it was originally an old chemist's counter. There is a beer garden at the front between the pub and the car park.

There is a very pleasant atmosphere about the place, and the landlord and staff are friendly and welcoming. It is a popular stopping place for walkers, but they do ask that groups should give advance warning if they will require food.

Food:
The menu is very varied and very interesting. There are various bar snacks, but also dishes such as moussaka, and prawns Greek style. They also do a range of vegetarian dishes.

Local Interest:
Bridford is an attractive little village near the eastern boundary of the National Park. There is fishing on the Kennick, Tottiford and Trenchford reservoirs a mile or two to the west, and also on the River Teign, a similar distance to the east. Riding is also available nearby.

Walks:
You can take paths and lanes to the reservoirs where there are some beautiful and undemanding walks. To the north a short walk along lanes and paths takes you to Steps Bridge, where you can follow the beautiful, wooded Teign Valley westwards.

Buckfastleigh

10. The Waterman's Arms

Map Reference:	736668
Open:	11.00-3.00, 5.00-11.00
Type:	Free house
On Draught:	Courage Best, Wadworth 6X, John Smith's,

	Worthington, Murphy's Stout, Strongbow Cider, Tinminers' Cider
Children:	In the family room and lounge
Dogs:	Yes
Food:	Midday and evening
Letter Box Stamp:	No
Parking:	A very small car park, but there is usually parking in the road
Accommodation:	2 rooms with en suite bathrooms
Facilities:	Family room with games - machines, darts and pool. There are a couple of tables outside.

Description:
There are several pubs in Buckfastleigh, but we find the Waterman's Arms the most congenial, despite its lack of parking and fairly basic bar food. It is a thirteenth-century inn, with beams, panelling and an open fire. It comprises an L-shaped room, one arm forming the bar and the other the lounge.

Situated near the town centre, it is a typical "local", with its groups of regulars. It has a pleasant atmosphere and both the bar staff and the local customers give visitors a friendly welcome. It is a popular meeting place for cavers.

The pub is said to be haunted by a woman, although no one seems to know who she was. She was most often seen in a room which is now part of the betting shop next door, but she has also appeared in a corner of the lounge, so you might be lucky!

Food:
They offer a range of standard bar food - jacket potatoes, soup and rolls, lasagne etc. - and some rather nice sweets.

Local Interest:
Buckfastleigh is a pleasant little town on the south-western edge of Dartmoor, with several tourist attractions. Nearby Buckfast Abbey is open to visitors and is one of the major "sights" of the area, attracting coachloads of people. There is also the Dart Valley Railway,

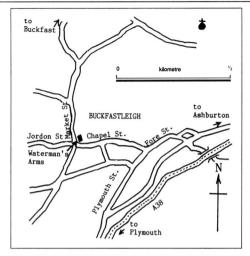

THE WATERMAN'S ARMS, BUCKFASTLEIGH

a delightful steam line which runs from Buckfastleigh to Totnes, and the Buckfast Butterfly Farm, with its wealth of exotic butterflies.

The town is a popular centre for cavers - the best caves are at Pridhamsleigh and at Baker's Pit near the church.

Walks:
There are several good walks around the town. To the north, beyond Buckfast, is Hembury Woods, a National Trust property. To the north-west there is a network of field and woodland paths and lanes to Scorriton and beyond to Holne. And to the west lies the Abbot's Way, leading to Dean Moor, the Avon Dam and the open moor. The Two Moors Way also passes to the west of the town.

Chagford

11. The Globe Inn

Map Reference:	701875
Open:	11.00-3.00, 6.00-11.00
Type:	Free house
On Draught:	Flowers IPA, Bass, Pedigree, Ansells, Whitbread Trophy, Guinness, Skol Lager, Carlsberg Export, Labatt's Lager, Copperhead Cider
Children:	Yes
Dogs:	Yes
Food:	Midday and evening
Letter Box Stamp:	Yes
Parking:	No car park, but plenty of parking outside
Accommodation:	5 rooms, all with en suite bathrooms
Facilities:	Restaurant. Function room. Pool, darts.

Description:
The Globe was a sixteenth-century coaching inn, but most of the present building dates back to about the eighteenth century, as much of the old pub was destroyed by fire. There are two bars. The lounge bar is nicely furnished, with upholstered bench seats and chairs and tables. It has two beautiful stone fireplaces, a large one with an open fire in it, and a smaller one which is purely decorative. The public bar is very much a "local", although this is the one that most walkers seem to prefer - perhaps because it looks less daunting when they walk in wet and muddy! The original Victorian decor has been retained, giving it a warm, snug, welcoming atmosphere, and there is a large Victorian fireplace. The restaurant is very pleasant, and also has an open fire.

Food:
There is a wide-ranging bar menu, including grills, salads, bar
32

The Bridge Inn, Ivybridge

The Castle Inn, Lydford
The Mountain Inn, Lutton

snacks and thirteen different types of jacket potato! There is also an à la carte restaurant menu.

Local Interest:
Chagford is a pretty little place just off the A382 between Moretonhampstead and Okehampton. Although it is a village in size, it is very proud of the fact that it is actually an ancient stannary town. It is very popular with tourists, and for a place of its size, it is surprisingly well provided with shops (and with pubs - there are three pubs and a hotel, all within a couple of hundred yards of each other).

Walks:
Chagford is a popular centre for walkers as well as tourists. The Two Moors Way passes just a few hundred yards to the north of the town, along the Teign Valley, and there are a number of paths to the east and south through woodland, moorland and river valleys. Meldon Hill and Nattadon Common, to the south, are popular hills to climb.

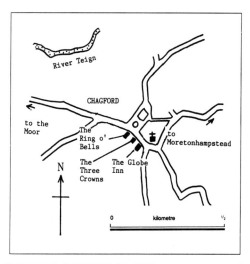

THE GLOBE INN, THE RING O'BELLS, THE THREE CROWNS, CHAGFORD

The Ring o'Bells, Chagford

12. The Ring o'Bells

Map Reference:	700875
Open:	11.00-3.00, 6.00-11.00
Type:	Free house
On Draught:	Bass, Burton, Palmers IPA, Dartmoor Best, Worthington Best, Ansells, Skol Lager, Carlsberg Export, Addlestone's Cider
Children:	In the dining area and garden
Dogs:	Yes
Food:	Midday and evening
Letter Box Stamp:	Yes
Parking:	No car park, but plenty of parking in the road
Accommodation:	No
Facilities:	Dining area. Beer garden. Darts.

Description:
There has been a pub on this site since 1160, but the present building dates back about 300 years. It is a very atmospheric place, with one long bar and a dining area at the back. The bar is nicely divided by wooden partitions and screens to form a series of semi-alcoves, and there is an open fire at one end. The walls are full of old photographs and prints. The dining area is very attractively decorated and furnished, with crisp linen on the tables. It also has a fireplace, and there is a pleasant little alcove at the end.

The pub has a long and somewhat varied history. The stannary court used to be held here in the days when Chagford was a stannary town, and the back part was used as a holding prison for prisoners on their way to Okehampton Assizes. Also at the back was the town morgue.

It is a popular pub with walkers and tourists alike, and the landlady is very welcoming.

Food:
There is a varied and very interesting menu, ranging from sandwiches to main meals. The same menu is used for the bar and the dining area.

Local Interest:
See previous entry.

Walks:
See previous entry.

13. The Three Crowns Hotel

Map Reference:	700875
Open:	11.00-11.00
Type:	Free house
On Draught:	Pedigree, Flowers Original, Whitbread Best, Whitbread Trophy, Murphy's Stout, Heineken Lager, Stella Artois Lager

The Three Crowns Hotel, Chagford

Children:	Yes
Dogs:	Yes
Food:	Midday and evening
Letter Box Stamp:	Yes
Parking:	Yes
Accommodation:	20 rooms, 18 with en suite bathrooms and 4 with four-poster beds. 4 cottages
Facilities:	Dining room. Function room. Beer garden. Darts, pool, skittles. Occasional folk evenings.

Description:
This two-star granite-built hotel dates from the thirteenth century when it was a manor house for John Whyddon. It was the Whyddon family (later Whiddon) which is said to have inspired R.D.Blackmore's classic, *Lorna Doone*. Indeed, in 1641 Mary Whiddon was shot dead by a jealous lover at the altar of Chagford Church, in much the same way as Lorna was shot in the novel. The pub's other claim to fame is that the poet and ardent Royalist Sidney Godolphin died here after being shot during the Civil War. Some say that his ghost still haunts the place.

The hotel has a beautiful stone porch in the front, which leads into the two bars. Both bars have bare stone walls, large stone fireplaces with open fires and low oak beams, and the lounge has fine mullioned windows. Both retain their traditional charm. A particular feature is the cartoons of the landlord and regulars which decorate the walls, all done by a local cartoonist.

The dining room leads off the lounge bar, and is spacious and comfortable. It is nicely arranged so that wherever you are sitting, you have the feeling of privacy. The small beer garden is at the back, with direct access to the car park.

This is a friendly pub, and walkers are welcomed.

Food:
There is a wide variety of food available, ranging from bar snacks to a full à la carte menu.

Local Interest:
See previous entry.

Walks:
See previous entry.

Christow

14. The Artichoke Inn

Map Reference:	832850
Open:	11.30-2.00, 7.00-11.00. Closed Tuesday and Thursday midday
Type:	Heavitree house
On Draught:	Marstons, Flowers IPA, Whitbread Best, Guinness, Stella Artois Lager, Heineken Lager, Strongbow Cider
Children:	In the dining area or garden
Dogs:	Yes

The Artichoke Inn, Christow

Food:	Midday and evening (except Tuesday midday and Thursday midday)
Letter Box Stamp:	Yes
Parking:	Yes
Accommodation:	2 rooms
Facilities:	Beer garden. Dining area. Juke box, darts, fruit machine.

Description:

A sixteenth-century inn, which is said to get its unusual name from the fact that the artichoke was introduced into Britain by the crusaders, many of whom visited this area as the guests of Lord Exmouth, one of the local landowners. It consists of three interconnected rooms, with a separate dining area off one of them. Full of atmosphere, there is a stone floor, low-beamed ceilings and a beautiful large stone fireplace with an open fire in winter. Walkers are welcomed, and the pub is particularly popular with letter-boxers. It is said to be haunted, although no one is sure by whom.

Food:

The food is excellent, with a wide range of dishes, including grills, fish, poultry and children's meals. Their home-made casseroles and pies are a speciality.

Local Interest:
Christow is a straggling village near the eastern boundary of the National Park, with some attractive buildings, but also some rather ugly developments. There is fishing on the Kennick, Tottiford and Trenchford reservoirs to the west, and also on the Teign to the east. The beautiful Canonteign Falls to the south are popular with tourists.

Walks:
There are several walks from Christow, but they all involve some lane walking. To the east lie the reservoirs, with beautiful and undemanding walks around them. To the north you can go up to Bridford and beyond to Steps Bridge and the lovely Teign Gorge. The route south is very pretty as you follow the Teign Valley, but it is mainly road walking.

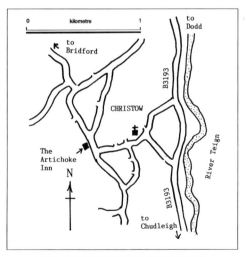

THE ARTICHOKE INN, CHRISTOW

Clearbrook

15. The Skylark

Map Reference:	657522
Open:	11.00-2.30, 6.30-11.00
Type:	Courage house
On Draught:	Directors, Courage Best, Guinness, Kronenbourg Lager, Fosters Lager, Dry Blackthorn Cider
Children:	In the children's room and garden
Dogs:	Yes
Food:	Midday and evening
Letter Box Stamp:	Pub stamp and seasonal stamps
Parking:	Yes. Ask about overnight parking.
Accommodation:	No
Facilities:	Children's room. Fruit machine. Pub sweatshirts available over the bar. Beer garden.

Description:
This is a cosy little eighteenth-century pub at the end of a row of miners' cottages. It started out as a farmhouse, but was soon converted into an ale house for the miners working at the nearby tin mines. There are two large open fires surrounded by brasswork and a collection of horsy bits and pieces, and there is an interesting collection of plates and dishes. There is just the one L-shaped bar. An interesting feature is the old oven set into the wall beside the fireplace. This is said to have been the communal oven for the whole village.

The children's room, called the Skylark's Nest, is outside, but it is heated, and is quite pleasant. It leads to the beer garden at the back.

Food:
All the food is home-made, and it is both delicious and reasonably

priced. But beware if you don't like garlic - it appears in most of the dishes! Dishes range from bar snacks to full meals, with a large selection of "specials" on the blackboard.

Local Interest:
Clearbrook is a small village in the south-western corner of Dartmoor. It consists mainly of a row of old miners' cottages which runs down the hill overlooking the moor to the south.

Walks:
There is a beautiful path along the River Meavy. It runs south to Shaugh Bridge (where you can continue eastwards along the Plym) and north towards Chubb Tor and Yelverton. You can reach the open moor to the east if you don't mind quite a lot of lane walking.

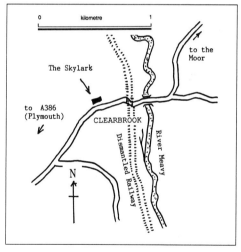

THE SKYLARK, CLEARBROOK

Cornwood

16. The Cornwood Inn

Map Reference:	605597
Open:	11.00-2.30, 7.00-11.00
Type:	Courage house
On Draught:	John Smith's, Directors, Symons Bitter, Courage Best, Beamish Stout, Kronenbourg Lager, Fosters Lager, Hofmeister Lager, Carlton LA, Dry Blackthorn Cider
Children:	If eating (otherwise ask)
Dogs:	In the public bar
Food:	Midday and evening
Letter Box Stamp:	Yes
Parking:	Yes. Ask about overnight parking.

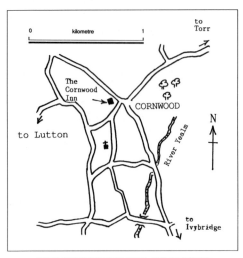

THE CORNWOOD INN, CORNWOOD

The Cornwood Inn, Cornwood

Accommodation:	No, but they can advise you on accommodation elsewhere
Facilities:	Pool, darts. Organ music on Friday nights, sing-alongs on Saturday nights.

Description:
This is a large pub, parts of which date back to before the eighteenth century. It was originally a coaching inn, and was enlarged about thirty years ago. It comprises two lounge bars, both comfortable but a little lacking in character. The lounge bar is L-shaped, with the eating area down a few steps on one side.

The landlord and staff are welcoming, and it is a pleasant place to stop but probably not one to seek out.

Food:
There is a wide range of food available, from bar snacks to steaks and grills, including vegetarian dishes.

Local Interest:
Cornwood is a pleasant village on the southern edge of Dartmoor,

in an area mainly of farmland and woods, leading up to open moorland.

Walks:
The walking in the area is interesting and varied. To the north-west lie Rook Gate, Shell Top and Lee Moor (owned by the National Trust). To the north-east, tracks and roads lead you to Stalldown Barrow and the Two Moors Way. And to the south-east are lanes and farm paths leading to Hanger Down.

Dousland

17. The Burrator Inn

Map Reference:	538689
Open:	11.00-11.00
Type:	Free house
On Draught:	Hicks, Burton, (subject to change - winter ales in winter), Bass, Carling Black Label Lager, Warsteiner Lager, Copperhead Cider, Gaymers Olde English Cyder
Children:	In the children's room, restaurant and garden
Dogs:	On a lead ('as long as the owners behave themselves!')
Food:	Midday and evening (sandwiches and ploughman's lunches midday only)
Letter Box Stamp:	Yes
Parking:	Yes. Ask about overnight parking.
Accommodation:	7 rooms, 5 with en suite bathrooms
Facilities:	Children's room. Garden and playground. Darts, pool, various machines. Good toilets.

Description:
A large, spacious Victorian pub, containing one long, continuous

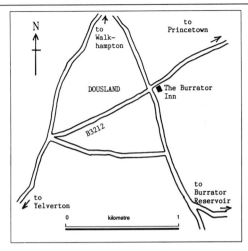

THE BURRATOR INN, DOUSLAND

bar divided into three, with the restaurant area at one end. The bar areas have a dark panelled effect, while the restaurant is beamed. There is a fireplace between the bars and the restaurant, with a stone and brick surround. With its carpeted floor and nicely padded seating, the overall effect is warm and welcoming. Even the background music is pleasantly unobtrusive.

Once rather grandly called the Manor Hotel, the pub served as an officers' mess during the Second World War, with the officers living across the road. It is a popular venue for walkers.

Food:
There is a range of bar snacks available, from sandwiches and ploughman's lunches (available only at midday) to basket meals and vegetarian dishes, as well as a full restaurant menu.

Local Interest:
A small village about 1¹/₄ miles (2km) east of Yelverton, Dousland itself does not have much to offer the visitor. However, there is fly fishing on the nearby Burrator Reservoir, after which the pub is named, and pony trekking in the vicinity.

Walks:
There are walks to and around Burrator Reservoir, a picturesque spot and popular picnic area almost completely surrounded by forest. To the east of the reservoir there are a number of tors to explore, depending on how energetic you are, from Sheeps Tor, the closest, to Down Tor, Combshead Tor and Higher Hartor Tor a little further afield. Beyond that, the options are almost endless, with open moorland to the east and north-east. The choice is more limited to the north of Dousland, but it is still possible, using paths and lanes, to reach Princetown this way, returning via the tors and moorland to the east, a round trip of about 14 miles (22km).

Drewsteignton

18. The Drewe Arms

Map Reference:	736908
Open:	10.30-2.30, 6.00-11.00
Type:	Whitbread house
On Draught:	Flowers IPA, Whitbread Keg, West Country Dry Cider
Children:	Yes
Dogs:	Yes
Food:	Midday only
Letter Box Stamp:	No
Parking:	In the village square outside the front door
Accommodation:	No
Facilities:	This is not the kind of pub to offer "facilities", although there is an "overflow" room at the back for local functions.

Description:
Dating from the seventeenth century, this is a totally unspoilt thatched village alehouse. Mrs Mudge (Aunty to the locals) is

The Drewe Arms, Drewsteignton

probably the oldest licensee in England (97 at the time of writing - 1992) and has been landlady since 1919. It was originally called the New Inn, and then changed its name to the Druid Arms. It became the Drewe Arms when Julius Drewe had Castle Drogo built nearby in the early part of this century.

There is no bar as such, just one small room, with the beer and cider being tapped in a kitchen-like room at the back. The front room has simple bench seats and a brick floor, and is decorated with old advertisements and photographs. The atmosphere is very informal, and the locals often wander through to the back to help themselves to drinks. Although it is beginning to look a little run down, it is well worth a visit, as it must be one of the few remaining examples of this kind of pub left unchanged. To go into it is like stepping back in history. It is very popular with walkers.

Food:
Only sandwiches are served, but they are rather special - great chunks of bread filled with ham.

Local Interests:
Drewsteignton is a small, picturesque thatched village near the northern edge of Dartmoor, with a delightful old church right next door to the pub. There is fishing on the river nearby, and Castle Drogo, built by Lutyens at the beginning of this century and now a National Trust property, is just down the road.

Walks:
There is a wide range of walks in the area, although you would have to go a long way to get to the open moor. The Two Moors Way goes through the village, and you can follow it north, out of Dartmoor to Hittsleigh and beyond, or south and west, past Castle Drogo and along the Teign Valley towards Chagford. There are paths leading east across rolling countryside to Crockernwell and south to the delights of Rectory Wood, Drewston Wood and Fingle Bridge on the River Teign.

THE DREWE ARMS, DREWSTEIGNTON

Dunsford

19. The Royal Oak

Map Reference:	812892
Open:	11.00-3.00, 6.30-11.00
Type:	Free house
On Draught:	Bass, Ruddles County, Ushers Best, Guinness, Fosters Lager, Carlsberg Export
Children:	Yes
Dogs:	Yes
Food:	Midday and evening (restaurant meals evening only, not Sundays)
Letter Box Stamp:	No
Parking:	Car park across the road
Accommodation:	8 rooms, 6 with en suite bathrooms
Facilities:	Restaurant. Garden. Pool room.

Description:
A red-brick Victorian inn built to replace one that burned down. Despite an uninspiring exterior, it is a pleasant, comfortable pub inside. There is a moderately sized bar in the centre, with a little restaurant to one side and a delightful lounge on the other and the pool room downstairs. The lounge has an imposing stone fireplace at one end. There is a garden to the rear.

It is the village "local", but both landlord and villagers give visitors a warm welcome. The local area is popular with walkers, and the pub serves them well - there are no problems about wet or muddy gear.

Food:
There is a good selection of appetising bar food, which changes from time to time, and full restaurant meals in the evening (except Sundays). They pride themselves on their home cooking and fresh local produce.

Local Interest:
Dunsford is a very pretty village of thatched cob cottages on the north-eastern edge of Dartmoor, about 7 miles (11km) from Exeter. The local church, built in the fifteenth century is worth a visit.

Walks:
There are some walks along lanes and paths to the north, east and west of the village, but the best walking in the area centres around Steps Bridge to the south (see next entry).

20. The Steps Bridge Inn

Map Reference:	804883
Open:	1.00-5.00, 7.30-10.30. Closed Tuesday and Wednesday evenings
Type:	Free house
On Draught:	Bass, Worthington Best, Murphy's Stout, Carlsberg Lager
Children:	Yes

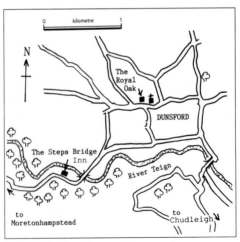

THE ROYAL OAK AND THE STEPS BRIDGE INN, DUNSFORD

Dogs:	No
Food:	Midday and evening (except Tuesday and Wednesday evenings)
Letter Box Stamp:	No
Parking:	Yes
Accommodation:	8 rooms, 4 with en suite bathrooms
Facilities:	Beer garden. Darts.

Description:

It is the position and outlook of this inn which makes it popular with walkers, for the pub itself is not particularly attractive. It is a fairly modern building right beside the River Teign at Steps Bridge, on the B3212 between Moretonhampstead and Dunsford. There are two small bars and a gravelled beer garden with direct access to the car park.

The real joy of the place is the large dining area overlooking a (private) garden and the river. It is at its best on a sunny day, but the different light effects on the trees and water make it a delightful view at any time.

Food:

There is a fairly standard range of bar food available, and they serve Devonshire cream teas.

Local Interest:

Steps Bridge crosses the River Teign just where it emerges from the steep, wooded Teign Gorge. The present bridge dates from 1816. There is a large public car park just next to the inn, with a Dartmoor Information Centre. It is a popular venue for family outings and even coach parties, as well as for the serious walker.

Walks:

There are some delightful and easy walks through Bridford and St Thomas Cleave woods on the south bank of the river, and through Dunsford Wood Nature Reserve on the north bank. The more adventurous can take the paths and lanes beyond the woods towards Bridford to the south and to Mardon Down to the west, and the river can be followed all the way up to Chagford.

Fingle Bridge

21. The Angler's Rest

Map Reference:	743899
Open:	11.00-3.00, 7.00-11.00. Evening opening Saturday only in winter
Type:	Free house
On Draught:	Thomas Hardy Country Ale, Eldridge Pope Best, Royal Oak, Guinness, Labatt's Lager, Kronenbourg Lager, Addlestone's Cider, Dry Blackthorn Cider
Children:	In the restaurant only
Dogs:	Yes
Food:	Midday and evening (evening opening Saturday only in winter)
Letter Box Stamp:	No
Parking:	Yes
Accommodation:	No
Facilities:	Restaurant. Beer garden. Function room. Postcards and fishing licences available from the bar. Shop selling cards, books, locally made foods, pottery, ice-creams and tourist items.

Description:
Built as a tea-room in 1897, this pub has been in the same family ever since - it is now in the hands of the fourth generation. The spacious bar overlooks the River Teign at one of its most beautiful points, Fingle Bridge. It has a beamed ceiling and two granite fireplaces, one containing a wood-burning stove. It is decorated with old angling equipment, specimen fish and fishing prints, and furnished with wheel-back chairs, bench seats and shining tables. There is also a large restaurant with a granite fireplace.

In summer, particularly when the sun is shining, the place to be is outside on the riverside terraces, watching the water flow by -

sheer bliss after a hard morning's walking!

Food:
There are separate midday and evening menus, with rather more substantial dishes in the evening. The choice is wide, ranging from soup and bar snacks to steak, fish and curry. The same food is served in the bar and the restaurant, except on Sundays when they serve a roast Sunday dinner in the restaurant. Devonshire cream teas are available.

Local Interest:
Fingle Bridge is an old sixteenth-century hump-backed stone bridge, one of the most photographed structures on Dartmoor. It crosses the Teign in a beautiful wooded gorge below Drewsteignton, and is a very popular place for family outings during the summer. There is fishing on the river, and Castle Drogo is a short walk away.

Walks:
The riverside walks around Fingle Bridge are among the best on Dartmoor - generally undemanding and delightfully wooded. You can follow the Teign for about 4¹/₂ miles (7.5km) in either direction.

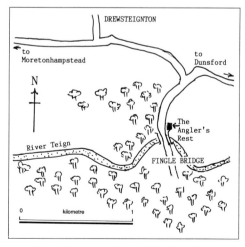

THE ANGLER'S REST, FINGLE BRIDGE

Grenofen

22. The Halfway House Inn

Map Reference:	491717
Open:	11.00-3.00, 6.00-11.00
Type:	Free house
On Draught:	Flowers IPA, Flowers Original, Boddingtons, Whitbread Best, Guinness, Heineken Lager, Stella Artois Lager, Dry Blackthorn Cider, Scrumpy Jack Cider (Occasional guest beers in summer)
Children:	In the dining room
Dogs:	In the public bar
Food:	Midday and evening
Letter Box Stamp:	No
Parking:	Yes. Ask about overnight parking
Accommodation:	5 rooms
Facilities:	Beer garden. Dining room. Pool, darts.

The Halfway House Inn, Grenofen

Description:

This pretty seventeenth-century coaching inn is right on the A386 Tavistock-Plymouth road. The original pub consisted only of what is now the public bar. What is now the lounge was originally shops and cottages.

The public bar is cosy, nicely carpeted, and with upholstered seats. It has a small gas fire. An interesting, if rather gruesome feature is the skull behind the bar. It is said to belong to a twelve-year-old girl. The lounge is a long room, decorated with interesting old photographs and prints, with the dining room at the end. It has an open fire and a pleasant, relaxing atmosphere.

This is a very friendly pub and they welcome walkers. There is a ghost, but even that is friendly - it goes in for practical jokes and pranks, switching things on and off, setting off the alarm etc.!

Food:

There is a wide selection of food, from bar snacks to full meals, including ten different vegetarian choices, and with some interesting specials on the board. There is a separate restaurant menu. A speciality is the traditional roast Sunday lunch.

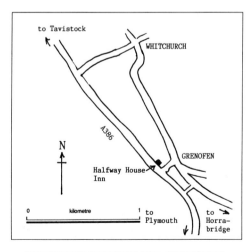

THE HALFWAY HOUSE INN, GRENOFEN

Local Interest:
Grenofen is a hamlet about 1 1/2 miles (2.5km) south-east of Tavistock, and just on the border of the National Park.

Walks:
There are no walks direct from Grenofen, and this is probably a pub for calling in at on your way to or from your walk. However, if you drive just a little way south there is lovely walking along the banks of the Walkham river and also through fields and woods both inside and outside the National Park.

Haytor Vale

23. The Rock Inn

Map Reference:	771772
Open:	11.00-2.30, 6.30-11.00
Type:	Free house
On Draught:	Rock Bitter (their own real ale), Royal Oak, Thomas Hardy Country Ale, Kronenbourg Lager, Labatt's Lager, Faust Export Lager, Red Rock Cider
Children:	In the children's eating area
Dogs:	No
Food:	Midday and evening
Letter Box Stamp:	Yes
Parking:	In the road
Accommodation:	10 rooms, 7 with en suite bathrooms
Facilities:	Children's eating area (which is also a non-smoking lounge), restaurant. Beer garden. Pub chocolates, sweets etc. available at the bar.

Description:
A lovely eighteenth-century coaching inn, very tastefully and
56

sympathetically decorated, with solid stone walls, exposed in places, and a number of little, semi-hidden corners. There is one oak-beamed main bar, decorated with plates, prints and figurines and nicely furnished with tables, padded chairs, settles and an old grandfather clock. It has two fireplaces. Across the passageway is the non-smoking lounge, which doubles as a children's eating area, and behind the bar a delightful little snug bar with room for no more than about eight or ten people.

The restaurant, which is only opened for Sunday lunches, is another beautiful room down a passage and past some more little nooks. A particularly nice feature is the small lounge, reserved for residents and restaurant guests, which is furnished with comfortable armchairs in which you can await your meal or enjoy your coffee. The very pleasant beer garden is across the road.

The inn is said to be haunted by a 200-year-old ghost called Belinda. She was apparently a serving wench at the inn who was having an affair with one of the coachmen. They were caught together by the coachman's wife, who beat poor Belinda to death on the stairs. So lifelike is her ghost that when Mrs Thatcher was

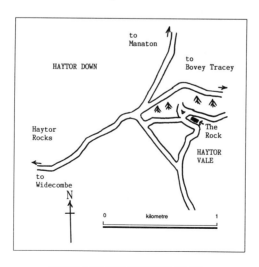

THE ROCK INN, HAYTOR VALE

staying at the inn a few years ago, one of her Special Branch detectives (not noted for their gullibility) saw it, thought it was an intruder, and shot it. Needless to say, the only result was a hole in the ceiling.

Walkers are welcomed at the Rock, but bear in mind that it is very tastefully decorated and carpeted, and a little consideration is appreciated - for example, waterproofs and muddy boots are best left in the foyer. It is also very much an "adult" rather than a family pub, although of course children are allowed into the non-smoking area.

Food:
There is an excellent and extensive menu. There are even special dishes for walkers - called Stilton Walkers and Cheddar Walkers, they consists of cheese and salad. The specialities include rabbit, beef and venison pie, and a range of vegetarian dishes.

Local Interest:
Haytor Vale is a little village at the foot of Haytor, one of the most famous of Dartmoor landmarks a few miles west of Bovey Tracey. Haytor is very popular with day-trippers and families, and also with rock climbers. Signs of the granite quarrying that used to take place here are all around, with disused quarries and the remains of the granite tramway which was used to transport the stone to the river for shipment. Across the Becka Valley from Haytor are two other popular climbing venues, Greator and Hound Tor, between which lie the ruins of a medieval village.

Walks:
There are walks to suit all tastes in this area, from strolls around the Haytor and Saddle Tor area (which tends to become a bit crowded in summer) to longer hikes across the valley to Hound Tor and even further to Bowerman's Nose.

The Palk Arms, Hennock

Hennock

24. The Palk Arms

Map Reference:	831809
Open:	12.00-2.30, 7.00-11.00
Type:	Free house
On Draught:	Dartmoor Best, Worthington Best, Ind Coope Pale Ale, Guinness, Carlsberg Lager, Lowenbrau Lager, Gaymers Olde English Cyder
Children:	In the family area and beer garden
Dogs:	Yes, except in the restaurant
Food:	Midday and evening
Letter Box Stamp:	Yes
Parking:	In the road
Accommodation:	2 rooms
Facilities:	Family area. Restaurant. Beer garden. Darts. Good toilets (there's a rare bread oven in the Ladies).

Description:

A delightful sixteenth-century pub (probably originally a church house), named after the Palk family who were major landowners in the area, with lands stretching from Haldon in the east to Moretonhampstead and Ashburton in the west. There is a charming and cosy bar in the front, and at the back a lounge with settles and rough pine tables, one of them beautifully carved. Forming part of the lounge, but half divided from it is a small family area, and at the end of the lounge a small restaurant area with magnificent views over the Teign Valley. There are open fires in both the lounge and the bar, and oak beams throughout.

The pub is set on a hill, and below the building itself is a pretty beer garden, with the same panoramic views as the restaurant. It is worth visiting for the view alone, quite apart from the traditional charm of the building and the warmth of the welcome you will receive. Not surprisingly, it is popular with walkers, but it is best visited at the end of your walk - if you go there before you set off you may not be able to drag yourself away from the view!

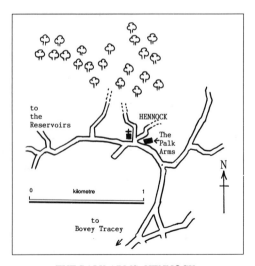

THE PALK ARMS, HENNOCK

Food:
The menu is not very extensive. It consists of light meals, starters, main courses and sweets - about four or five dishes in each category - with a few daily specials. But what there is, is well cooked and very good value for money.

Local Interest:
Hennock is a small village north-east of Bovey Tracey. There is not much of interest in the village itself, but nearby are the linked reservoirs of Kennick, Tottiford and Trenchford, which are very popular with anglers, picnickers and walkers.

Walks:
You can walk from the pub north-west to the reservoirs, and there are beautiful and undemanding walks around the reservoirs themselves. It is not, of course, real moorland walking, but no less pleasant for all that. You can also follow paths and lanes westwards to Lustleigh and the Cleave beyond.

Hexworthy

24a. The Forest Inn

Map Reference:	655726
Open:	11.00-3.00, 6.00-11.00
Type:	Free house
On Draught:	Palmers, Dartmoor Best, Wadworth 6X, Ansells, Worthington Best, Murphy's Stout, Castlemaine Lager, Carlsberg Lager, Tinminers' Cider
Children:	In the food areas only
Dogs:	Yes
Food:	Midday and evening
Letter Box Stamp:	Yes. The hobby of letter-boxing is said to have originated here.

Parking:	Yes
Accommodation:	10 rooms, 8 with en suite bathrooms
Facilities:	Beer garden. Restaurant area. Fishing licences available from the pub.

Description:

An old coaching inn stood on this site, but it was destroyed by fire in 1914. The present inn is therefore relatively new, having been completed in 1916. It is a large pub, with an interesting layout of four interconnected rooms on an open-plan system, with the bar in one room and the restaurant in another. There is also a comfortable lounge area with deep armchairs and an open fire, and a fourth room for bar food; both of these rooms lead into the garden. All four rooms are tastefully decorated and furnished.

The pub was closed for some time, and has only recently re-opened, so there may well be some changes in its appearance and layout. The staff are very friendly, and that is unlikely to change. Walkers are made very welcome.

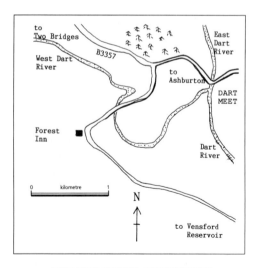

THE FOREST INN, HEXWORTHY

Food:
There is a wide range of imaginative bar snacks and restaurant meals, and an extensive wine list.

Local Interest:
This is a good centre for a number of outdoor pursuits, including pony trekking, canoeing, fishing and rock climbing. Dartmeet, a popular picnic spot, is nearby.

Walks:
The walking in this area is superb and very varied. The choice of routes is almost endless, and it is possible to combine delightful river valleys, beautiful farms and woodlands and wild open moorland in the same walk. There are four rivers in the area - the Dart, its two components the East and West Dart and the Swincombe - and most of the walks involve crossing one or more of them. After heavy rain, these crossings can be tricky, so it is worth checking on the level of the rivers before setting out.

Holne

25. The Church House Inn

Map Reference:	706695
Open:	12.00-2.30, 6.30-11.00
Type:	Free house
On Draught:	Palmers IPA, Blackawton, Blackawton 44, Murphy's Stout, Carlsberg Export, Addlestone's Cider, Tinminers' Cider
Children:	In the Kingsley Room
Dogs:	Yes
Food:	Midday and evening
Letter Box Stamp:	No
Parking:	In the road or the free public car park just down the road

Accommodation:	7 bedrooms, 4 with en suite bathrooms
Facilities:	Restaurant. Residents' sitting room with books and writing materials. Washing and drying facilities for those staying more than one night. Souvenir postcards.

Description:

An attractive fourteenth-century inn which was probably built as a resting place for visiting clergy and worshippers. It is a very traditional pub with beams, leaded windows and a timber partition wall between the bars and the Kingsley Room. There are two small interconnecting bars furnished with scrubbed tables and wheel-back chairs. The Kingsley Room, which leads on from the bars, serves as a lounge-cum-family room. There are open fires in the Kingsley Room and one of the bars. Although there is no garden as such, there are benches outside, and a small lawn on which to sit and watch the world go by.

The proprietors have been very successful in retaining the traditional atmosphere of the inn, which attracts a nice mix of locals

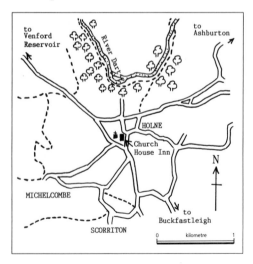

THE CHURCH HOUSE INN, HOLNE

and visitors. It is very popular with walkers of all standards, and they have no objection to muddy boots and dripping clothes.

Food:
The food here is excellent - all home-made from fresh ingredients. A good selection of bar food is available, from ploughman's lunches and jacket potatoes to salads and fish dishes, as well as restaurant meals. The sweets are delicious and they have a superb variety of ice-creams. Most diets can be catered for, and they pride themselves on the fact that they do not serve chips with anything. Sunday lunches are a speciality and they do packed lunches for residents.

Local Interest:
Holne is a pleasant village nestling in the lee of the south-east edge of the moor just above the River Dart about 3 miles (5km) from Ashburton. The Dart is popular with canoeists, and there is salmon and trout fishing in season. There are riding stables nearby.

Walks:
This is a very popular area for walkers. There are walks to suit all tastes, from a delightful short stroll through Holne Woods (National Trust) along the river to New Bridge, to longer routes west to Holne Moor and north-west to Venford Reservoir. The Two Moors Way passes the door of the inn.

Horndon

26. The Elephant's Nest

Map Reference:	518800
Open:	11.30-2.30, 6.30-11.00
Type:	Free house
On Draught:	Hicks, Boddingtons, Palmers Best, Guinness, Carlsberg Lager, Holsten Export, Bulmers Traditional Cider (Plus guest beers)
Children:	In the extension

Dogs:	On a lead
Food:	Midday and evening (3-course meals evenings only)
Letter Box Stamp:	Yes
Parking:	Yes. Ask about overnight parking.
Accommodation:	2 rooms
Facilities:	Beer garden. Darts, dominoes, cards.

Description:
This is a sixteenth-century building, but has only been a pub for about 100 years - it was previously miners' cottages. It consists of one bar with a two-room extension off it, and several little nooks and alcoves. The stone walls are stained with age, and there is a large open fire and a stone floor, so there is no problem about muddy feet on a nice carpet! The low-beamed wooden ceiling has the name of the pub written on it in several languages, and there is also an interesting collection of foreign banknotes. It is a very cosy

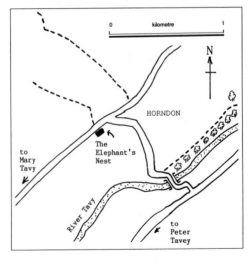

THE ELEPHANT'S NEST, HORNDON

place, with a warm, friendly atmosphere. There is a beer garden to the front.

The pub gets its unusual name from the enormous size of a previous landlord.

Food:
There is a wide selection of meals of all kinds, from snacks to main meals. Three-course meals are available only in the evenings.

Local Interest:
Horndon is a very small village to the east of Mary Tavy. There is not much of local interest except walking!

Walks:
There is a wide variety of walking here. You can take a gentle stroll down to the River Tavy and through Creason Wood, wander up to Kingsett Down and Wheal Jewell Reservoir, or go further afield on to the moor. If you are going on to the moor, you should check firing times before you go, as this area of Dartmoor is a military range. There are any number of circular routes which will combine a variety of scenery and terrain.

Horrabridge

27. The Leaping Salmon

Map Reference:	513700
Open:	11.00-11.00
Type:	Courage house
On Draught:	Directors, Courage Best, John Courage, John Smith's, Hofmeister Lager, Fosters Lager, Kronenbourg Lager, Dry Blackthorn Cider
Children:	In the garden
Dogs:	On a lead
Food:	Midday and evening

Letter Box Stamp:	No
Parking:	Yes. Ask about overnight parking
Accommodation:	No
Facilities:	Beer garden with kiddies' cabin. Pool, darts, euchre, dominoes.

Description:

A large pub with a bar, a lounge and a restaurant area. There are two granite fireplaces in the lounge and one in the bar, although only the ones in the lounge are used. The bar is a spacious room with plenty of seating and with a pool table in the centre. The lounge contains an old water-wheel (no longer in use), in a nice little area with fish tanks. The lounge is on two levels, the lower of which is furnished with wheel-back chairs, and the upper with padded seating. The bar itself is interesting, as it is made of old barrels called kilderkins.

The pub used to be known as the Starving Pig because one of the previous landlords kept pigs and didn't feed them enough. One of the pigs regularly broke out and came into the bar looking for food! The locals also used to bring their ferrets in, let them loose one at a

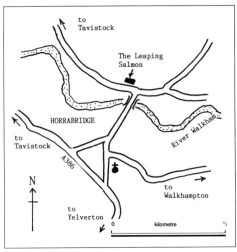

THE LEAPING SALMON, HORRABRIDGE

time on the pool table and bet on which hole they would emerge from. It's that kind of place! It is a popular starting or finishing point for walkers.

Food:
There is a wide range of bar snacks, from sandwiches and pasties to salads, pizzas and lasagne. There is also an extensive à la carte menu, which is very good value. A speciality is their mixed grill - ten different items on one plate. Finishing it is something of a feat, and it is best tried *after* your walk rather than before!

Local Interest:
Horrabridge is a fairly large village on the western edge of Dartmoor. There are some attractive old buildings, but also some rather unattractive new ones. The pub is in a delightful setting, with the River Walkham flowing by just opposite its door. There is salmon and trout fishing in the river.

Walks:
This is a little-frequented but delightful part of Dartmoor. There are walks in all directions (including south-west, out of the National Park to Buckland Monachorum), but the best walking is north-eastwards. There is a pleasant circular walk in that direction to Sampford Spiney and back, or you can extend your route beyond Sampford Spiney to Merrivale and on to the high moor. If you are going beyond Merrivale, remember that you will be entering a military firing range, and check the firing times.

Ivybridge

28. The Bridge Inn

Map Reference:	637563
Open:	12.00-11.00
Type:	Courage house
On Draught:	Courage Best, John Smith's, Beamish Stout,

	Fosters Lager, Kronenbourg Lager, Dry Blackthorn Cider
Children:	"Tolerated"!
Dogs:	"Welcomed"
Food:	No
Letter Box Stamp:	No
Parking:	In the road or the public car park across the road
Accommodation:	No
Facilities:	Beer garden. Pool, darts, pub games.

Description:
This inn used to be the village bakery, and there is still a leat running underground from the River Erme, which cools the cellar. There is one bar divided into three areas. The first, public bar area has bare stone walls and a stone floor, and from there one walks through to the second area, which has a wooden floor, and then through to the lounge, with a carpeted floor, upholstered seating and panelled walls and ceiling.

It feels more like a village inn than a town pub. It has a cosy atmosphere, with old guns and other knick-knacks on the walls and beams and beautiful open fireplaces, some of which are in use while others are purely decorative. Despite the lack of food, it is a good place to stop for refreshment, and is close to the start of the Two Moors Way and routes to the moor.

Local Interest:
Ivybridge is a fairly large town just outside the National Park boundary to the south. The town boasts a large new leisure centre, with both indoor and outdoor swimming pools and squash and badminton courts.

Walks:
Ivybridge is where the Two Moors Way starts, and you can follow this interesting route as far as you wish - all the way to Exmoor if you feel so inclined! There are also some beautiful shorter walks, in

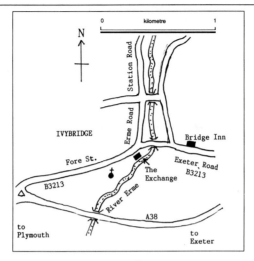

THE BRIDGE INN AND THE EXCHANGE, IVYBRIDGE

particular up the Erme Valley, around Henlake Down or further
north to Hanger Down. A lovely and varied circular route takes you
up the Erme Valley, across through Harford to meet the Two Moors
Way, and back to Ivybridge along the Way.

29. The Exchange

Map Reference:	635563
Open:	11.00-11.00
Type:	Courage house
On Draught:	Directors, Courage Best, Guinness, Miller Lite, Dry Blackthorn Cider
Children:	In the lounge area
Dogs:	On a lead
Food:	Midday and evening
Letter Box Stamp:	No

The Exchange, Ivybridge

Parking: No

Accommodation: 5 rooms, all with en suite bathrooms

Facilities: Pool, darts, euchre

Description:
This is a large pub overlooking the river, with a single L-shaped bar. One arm of the L forms the public bar area, and the other the very spacious lounge and eating area. It still has the old stone white-painted walls, decorated with an enormous set of bellows and some interesting farm implements. There is a lovely view down to the river.

It is a very friendly pub, with a comfortable, welcoming atmosphere.

Food:
There is a wide range of food, from bar snacks to restaurant meals, including a variety of vegetarian dishes.

Local Interest:
See previous entry.

Walks:
See previous entry.

Lustleigh

30. The Cleave

Map Reference:	785813
Open:	11.00-2.30, 6.00-11.00
Type:	Free house
On Draught:	Bass, Whitbread Best, Flowers IPA, Murphy's Stout, Heineken Lager
Children:	In the family room and garden
Dogs:	Yes
Food:	Midday and evening
Letter Box Stamp:	No
Parking:	Small car park, with additional parking in the road. Overnight parking for residents only.
Accommodation:	3 bedrooms, 2 bathrooms
Facilities:	Garden. Family room, with darts and video games. Dining room. Good toilets.

Description:
"Cleave" means valley, and the inn is named after Lustleigh Cleave, a very attractive part of the Bovey Valley which lies to the west of Lustleigh itself. It is a fifteenth-century thatched inn in the heart of the village, with a small but cosy bar and a dining room at the front, and a larger but less attractive bar and a family room at the back. There is a vast inglenook fireplace in the front bar, and in the dining room the huge granite walls have been exposed. The family room is not the kind of bleak, poorly decorated place one finds in so many pubs, with plastic-covered tables and uncomfortable chairs, but a nice-looking, comfortable, welcoming room. The rear bar is pleasant, but not as cosy as the front one, and is used mainly for "overflow" purposes.

Hardly surprisingly, this is a popular pub with walkers, especially at weekends, when whole families come to walk along the Cleave and explore the tors above the village. The old world charm, the good food, the delightful garden and the superb setting all combine to make it an ideal resting place. On a sunny summer's day, after a good long ramble, there is nothing nicer than to relax with a drink in the beautiful garden, looking out on the old church and the village green.

Food:
There is a good selection of food, from imaginative bar meals to restaurant menus. There are separate menus for lunch and dinner.

Local Interest:
Lying about 4 miles (6km) north of Bovey Tracey, Lustleigh is one of the most attractive villages in Devon - everyone's idea of what an English village should look like. The ancient church, thatched inn and old cottages cluster round the village green in traditional style.

The church, which dates from the thirteenth to the sixteenth

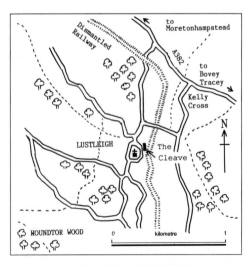

THE CLEAVE, LUSTLEIGH

centuries, is worth a visit. It contains a rather attractive screen from the time of Mary I.

Walks:
There are many delightful walks in the area, particularly in and above the Bovey Valley. One of the most popular is the circuit of Lustleigh Cleave. It is classified by some guides as an easy walk, but this is somewhat misleading, as there are several quite steep ascents. It is therefore not a walk for the unfit. You can also walk across the valley to Manaton and Hound Tor, or follow paths and lanes to North Bovey.

Lutton

31. The Mountain Inn

Map Reference:	597594
Open:	11.00-3.00, 6.00-11.00
Type:	Free house
On Draught:	Bass, Wadworth 6X, Mountain Inn Strong Ale (their own brew), Dartmoor Strong, Tetley, Murphy's Stout, Castlemaine Lager, Carlsberg Export, Inch's Stonehouse Cider
Children:	In the children's room
Dogs:	No
Food:	Midday and evening
Letter Box Stamp:	2 stamps
Parking:	Yes. Ask about overnight parking.
Accommodation:	No
Facilities:	Children's room. Darts, euchre, various pub games. Quiz nights and conker nights.

Description:
This pleasant inn has been in existence for about 200 years, but the building is even older. It was formed by converting two cottages,

one of which was already a cider and ale house. It did not get its name from the fact that it is on a mountain, but from a local seventeenth-century squire, Lord Mourtain.

It has stone walls and low, beamed ceilings. There is a small bar with an open fire and rush matting on the stone floor, and a comfortable lounge furnished with tables and chairs, a grandmother clock and an old carved chest. The bar is a warm, cosy place, while the lounge has more of the atmosphere of a dining room.

There is a large, attractive vine at the front of the building, with tables set out underneath it. Walkers are welcome, and the landlord loves a game of spoof.

Food:
There is a range of bar snacks, as well as specials on the blackboard. The beef is particularly good.

Local Interest:
Lutton is a pleasant little village just outside the southern boundary of the National Park. The Dartmoor Wildlife Park is just down the road, and there is pony trekking nearby.

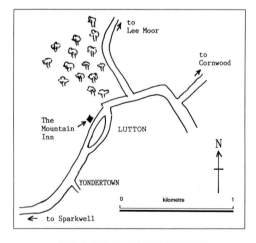

THE MOUNTAIN INN, LUTTON

Walks:
To the west of Lutton lie the disfiguring china clay works, but there are footpaths that skirt them and lead to Crownhill Down. You can either go south-west towards Sparkwell and then north-west via the remains of various mines and clay workings, or north and then west via Broomage Wood. North-east lies Dartmoor proper, with paths to Hanger Down one way and Shell Top the other.

Lydford

32. The Castle Inn

Map Reference:	509848
Open:	11.00-3.00, 6.00-11.00
Type:	Free house
On Draught:	Dartmoor Best, Palmers Best, Burtons Ale, Guinness, Lowenbrau Lager, Castlemaine Lager, Gaymers Olde English Cyder
Children:	In the restaurant and snug
Dogs:	In the public bar
Food:	Midday and evening
Letter Box Stamp:	2 stamps
Parking:	Yes. Ask about overnight parking.
Accommodation:	8 rooms, 6 with en suite bathrooms, one with a four-poster bed
Facilities:	Beer garden. Restaurant. Darts, cards, cribbage, Trivial Pursuit.

Description:
A beautiful traditional sixteenth-century inn, full of charm and character, with vines and climbing plants on the front. As the name suggest, it is next to Lydford Castle. It was featured in the film *The Hound of the Baskervilles* as the Admiral Blake Inn.

The public bar is small and comfortable with a slate flag floor and a large open fire. The restaurant is decorated with an interesting assortment of plates and prints, and furnished with magnificent old wooden settles. Leading off the restaurant is the snug, a cosy little room with upholstered seats and a carpeted floor. There is a large and attractive beer garden.

Food:
There is a daily menu of bar snacks on the board, and both à la carte and table d'hôte menus for the restaurant, all freshly cooked and including local fish, meat and game.

Local Interest:
Lydford is an attractive village on the western edge of the National Park. Its two most famous landmarks are the castle, which is well worth a visit, and Lydford Gorge, a beautiful and popular National Trust property, containing the spectacular White Lady Waterfall, which is on the edge of the town.

Walks:
It would be a great pity to visit Lydford without seeing the magnificent wonderland of rocks, wood and water that is Lydford Gorge. There is a relatively short and easy circuit. Note that access is restricted in the winter months.

Apart from the Gorge, there are paths leading to the A386 and the moors beyond. But since this is a military range you should check on firing times before venturing too far.

33. The Dartmoor Inn

Map Reference:	523852
Open:	11.00-11.00
Type:	Free house
On Draught:	Bass, Tinners, H.S.B., Worthington Best, Guinness, Murphy's Stout, Tennents Pilsner, Tennents Extra, Inch's Stonehouse Cider

Children:	In the children's area
Dogs:	On a lead
Food:	Midday and evening
Letter Box Stamp:	Yes
Parking:	Yes. Ask about overnight parking.
Accommodation:	3 rooms
Facilities:	Darts, cards, shove ha'penny, dominoes. Children's room.

Description:

There has been an inn on this site for some 700 years, but the present building dates back to the sixteenth century. There are two bars, both with low ceilings, wood panelling and massive fireplaces, and both nicely carpeted. Although there is plenty of room, the overall impression is of a warm, cosy atmosphere.

The inn originally served packhorse drivers, and was a useful

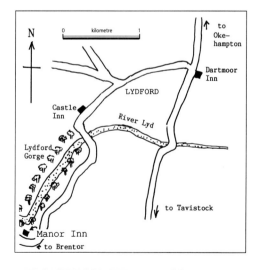

THE CASTLE INN, THE DARTMOOR INN AND
THE MANOR INN, LYDFORD

halfway house for those of Drake's sailors and officers who lived in North Devon. It was here that Salvation Yeo, Bosun to Captain Amos Leigh, killed the King of the notorious Gubbins tribe, an event immortalised by Charles Kingsley in *Westward Ho!*.

Food:
There is a large and varied choice of home-made dishes, from snacks to main meals, including children's meals and vegetarian dishes. There are also daily specials.

Local Interest:
The pub is on the A386 between Tavistock and Okehampton, near the western edge of the National Park. Lydford, with its castle, and Lydford Gorge, with its spectacular scenery and waterfall are about a mile (1.5km) or so away.

Walks:
There is access to the moor via a track running east from the pub. Brat Tor is about a mile (1.5km) up the track, and beyond that you can walk in almost any direction, as this is open moorland. It is rough and wild, so take care, particularly in bad weather. It is also part of the military range, so check on firing times before venturing too far.

34. The Manor Inn

Map Reference:	502831
Open:	11.00-11.00
Type:	Free house
On Draught:	Bass, Butcombe Bitter, Worthington Best, Toby, Guinness, Carling Black Label Lager, Tennents Pilsner, Tennents Extra, Dry Blackthorn Cider
Children:	Yes
Dogs:	Yes
Food:	Midday and evening

The Dartmoor Inn, Merrivale

The Ring of Bells, North Bovey

The Peter Tavy Inn, Peter Tavy
The East Dart Hotel, Postbridge

The Manor Inn, nr Lydford

Letter Box Stamp: Yes
Parking: Yes. Ask about overnight parking.
Accommodation: 8 rooms, all with en suite bathrooms
Facilities: Beer garden. Function room. Darts, pool, cards.

Description:
A large eighteenth-century house, which was converted into a pub about 150 years ago. There are two main bars, both with partly exposed stone walls and large fireplaces with log fires. The lounge bar has a homely, friendly atmosphere, with a stone floor and attractive pine furniture. Just off the lounge bar is a small, cosy snug with a carpeted floor. The other main bar is the public bar, which is a small room which serves as a games room, with the pool table and darts board.

Food:
There is a range of bar snacks and main meals, including vegetarian dishes, with a wide range of daily specials on the board. Prices are very reasonable, and all the food is home-cooked. Cream teas are served.

Local Interest:
The pub is at the southern end of Lydford Gorge, just by the White Lady Waterfall entrance. The main centre of interest is, of course, the Gorge, but the pub also has fishing rights on the River Lyd, and there is pony trekking nearby.

Walks:
See entry for the Castle Inn.

Manaton

35. The Kestor Inn

Map Reference:	757807
Open:	11.00-2.30, 6.30-11.00
Type:	Free house
On Draught:	Wadworth 6X, Blackawton 44, Flowers Original, Bentley's, Guinness, Murphy's Stout, Heineken Lager, Stella Artois Lager, Woodpecker Cider, Scrumpy Jack Cider
Children:	In the family room, restaurant and beer garden
Dogs:	Yes
Food:	Midday and evening (reduced menu at midday on Sundays and bank holidays)
Letter Box Stamp:	Yes
Parking:	Yes. Ask about overnight parking.
Accommodation:	2 rooms
Facilities:	Restaurant. Family room. Beer garden with children's play area. Fruit machines.

Description:
This is a relatively modern pub, built early this century. You go through the family room, nicely furnished with benches and tables, and then into the large bar. This is divided into interesting alcoves

and areas by stone pillars, and is furnished with comfortable upholstered bench seats, tables and wheel-back chairs. There is an open fire at one end, and an interesting feature is the fountain in the corner. The restaurant leads off the bar, and is a delightful room with large picture windows, and the beer garden is below it, with a children's play area alongside.

This is a popular pub with walkers, both because of its situation and because of its letter-box stamps.

Food:
There is a wide range of bar snacks and main meals, plus an imaginative variety of daily "specials" from the blackboard. They do very good Sunday roasts.

Local Interest:
Manaton is a small, rather sprawling village north-west of Bovey Tracey. It is not far from the beautiful and very popular Becky Falls, a favourite place for family outings.

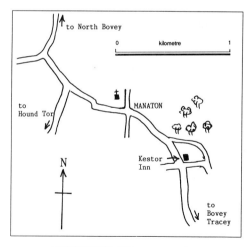

THE KESTOR INN, MANATON

Walks:
There are walks of all kinds and in every direction from Manaton, many of them circular. The well-known landmark Bowerman's Nose lies to the west of the village, with paths leading on from there to Hameldown Tor and beyond, or southwards to Hound Tor. To the south is the delightful valley of the Becka Brook, with a fairly easy walk through Houndtor Wood. To the east there are a number of paths leading to Lustleigh Cleave and to the north you can follow paths and lanes to North Bovey and Moretonhampstead.

Meavy

36. The Royal Oak

Map Reference:	673540
Open:	11.00-2.30, 6.00-11.00
Type:	Free house
On Draught:	Boddingtons, Bass, Castle Eden, Flowers IPA, Guinness, Murphy's Stout, Heineken Lager, Stella Artois Lager, Scrumpy Jack Cider, Bulmers Traditional Cider, Dry Blackthorn Cider
Children:	On the green only
Dogs:	Yes
Food:	Midday and evening
Letter Box Stamp:	2 stamps
Parking:	In the village
Accommodation:	No
Facilities:	Darts, card games. National Park Information Centre.

Description:
A friendly sixteenth-century village pub with a small green to the front. There are two beautiful oak-beamed bars - a small, cosy public

bar with a large open log fire, and a larger L-shaped lounge bar with plenty of tables and upholstered settles and stools. Both are full of atmosphere and tradition.

The pub is named after the old oak tree which is just outside and is about 500 years old, although why it should be "royal" is uncertain. Before the church was built, there was a preaching stone by the green, from which itinerant preachers would give their sermons, and tradition has it that the tree was planted to give shelter to the preachers' audience.

At one end of the pub is an old wood shed with a large solid door. Cut into the door is a slot about the size of a post box, which slopes down into the shed. Opinions differ as to what it was for. Half the village believe that it was used to keep the pub pig in, with the slot being used to push food through. The other half claim that lepers were kept there, and the feeding slot sloped to prevent them putting their hands through and contaminating the rest of the village.

It is a very popular pub with walkers, particularly in summer, and in good weather it is delightful to be able to take one's drink out on to the green.

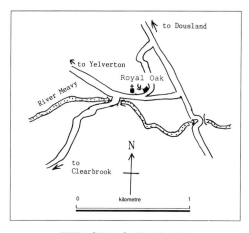

THE ROYAL OAK, MEAVY

Food:
The food is excellent. The menu is constantly changing, but there is always a wide variety of dishes, ranging from sandwiches to full meals.

Local Interest:
Meavy is an attractive little village on the western side of Dartmoor, near Yelverton, and quite close to Burrator Reservoir. The Ford, a very pleasant area for picnics, is not far away.

Walks:
Meavy is an ideal centre for walking - there are paths in almost every direction. To the north lies Yennadon Down, Sharpitor and Walkhampton Common; to the north-east is Burrator Reservoir and beyond that the open moor around Foxtor Mires; to the east the Abbot's Way leads to Buckfastleigh; and to the south there are paths and lanes towards Shaugh Prior.

Merrivale

37. The Dartmoor Inn

Map Reference:	549752
Open:	Summer : 11.00-3.00, 6.00-11.00. Winter: 11.00-2.30, 6.30-11.00
Type:	Free house
On Draught:	Bass, Flowers IPA, Merrivale, Worthington Best, Tennents Extra, Stella Artois Lager, Dry Blackthorn Cider, Autumn Gold Cider
Children:	In the children's room
Dogs:	On a lead
Food:	Midday and evening
Letter Box Stamp:	3 pub stamps and occasional "specials"
Parking:	Yes. Ask about overnight parking.

Accommodation:	4 rooms. Camping in the field alongside (but please ask first).
Facilities:	Children's room. Darts, cards, dominoes.

Description:

This is a very comfortable old inn. There are two interconnected bars with a large stone fireplace between them, and an open fire in each room, with wooden settles to the side. The white plastered walls and low wooden beams give it a warm, snug atmosphere, and there is an interesting collection of pots, mugs and plates of all kinds. It is very popular with walkers, especially letter-boxers because of the variety of stamps. It is famous for its country wines, straight from the wood.

The pub is said to be haunted by a ghost called Mary who died here before the war.

Food:

They have a wide range of bar snacks and main meals and daily specials are available at lunchtime in the winter.

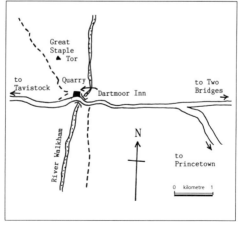

THE DARTMOOR INN, MERRIVALE

Local Interest:
Merrivale is simply a place on the map, on the B3357 between Two Bridges and Tavistock - there is no village as such. But there are a number of hut circles close by, and stone rows which are sometimes called the Plague Market because farmers used to leave produce there to be collected by the citizens of plague-ridden Tavistock in 1625. There is also pony trekking in the vicinity.

The pub is very high, and when it is clear you can see Plymouth Sound, and even the Eddystone Light, some thirty miles away.

Walks:
The walking here is superb. To the north lies the wild open moor. If you are venturing in that direction, especially in bad weather, take extra care. Also remember to check on firing time; this part of the moor is a military range. To the south is more gentle farm and woodland, with paths leading to Sampford Spiney and Walkhampton Common. A circular walk which combines the best of both takes you down the wooded Walkham Valley, then across towards Walkhampton Common, and back across open moorland via King's Tor.

Moretonhampstead

38. The White Hart Hotel

Map Reference:	753860
Open:	11.00-11.00
Type:	Free house
On Draught:	Bass, Dartmoor Best, Whitbread Trophy, Tetley, John Bull, Carlsberg Export, Skol Lager, Castlemaine Lager, Luscombe Dry Scrumpy
Children:	In the lounge, family room and beer garden
Dogs:	Yes
Food:	Midday and evening
Letter Box Stamp:	Yes

Parking:	Yes. Overnight parking for residents.
Accommodation:	20 rooms, all with en suite bathrooms
Facilities:	Beer garden. Family room. Conference room. Dining room. Drying room. Games.

Description:

The White Hart is a two-star hotel, dating back to the sixteenth century, right in the middle of Moretonhampstead. It was once a posting inn and the London-Plymouth coaches stopped here. During the Napoleonic Wars it was also a meeting place for French officer prisoners of war out on parole from Dartmoor Prison.

There are two bars: a cosy public bar with a beamed ceiling and horse brasses, furnished with seats and settles; and an elegant lounge, consisting of two communicating rooms, nicely decorated and furnished with wicker armchairs and low tables. The public bar is a popular meeting place for locals, while the lounge is used more by residents and visitors. The dining room has a charm of its own, and contains some beautiful pieces of furniture, while the family room is plain but pleasant. The beer garden is actually just a

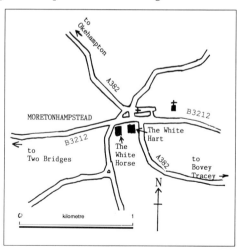

THE WHITE HART AND THE WHITE HORSE,
MORETONHAMPSTEAD

*The White Hart Hotel,
Moretonhampstead*

courtyard and has no view, but it is nevertheless a pleasant place to sit.

This is a friendly, homely hotel offering a warm welcome to all visitors. Walkers are made to feel at home, and the drying room is a real boon.

Food:
There is an extensive menu, ranging from simple bar snacks to à la carte restaurant dishes and a range of set menus - there really is something to suit every taste, including vegetarian dishes. Fresh local produce is used whenever possible.

Local Interest:
Moretonhampstead is a small town at the junction of the Bovey Tracey-Okehampton and Pricetown-Exeter roads. The main interest for visitors lies on the moor itself, but there are some attractive sixteenth-century almshouses and a fourteenth-century church.

Walks:
This is not the wild open moorland one finds further west, but an area of farms and fields. Walking is therefore more restricted, but there are nevertheless pleasant walks to the north to the prehistoric hill fort of Cranbrook Castle and to the south to North Bovey. This southern walk can be extended via lanes and paths towards Manaton.

39. The White Horse

Map Reference: 753860

Open: 11.00-3.00, 5.30-11.00 (all day in summer)

Type:	Free house
On Draught:	John Smith's, Courage Best, Fosters Lager, Kronenbourg Lager, Miller Lite, Carlton LA
Children:	Yes
Dogs:	Yes
Food:	Midday and evening
Letter Box Stamp:	Yes
Parking:	Free public car park round the corner
Accommodation:	9 rooms, 3 with en suite bathrooms
Facilities:	Restaurant. Pool, darts, video games.

Description:

A delightful seventeenth-century pub with bare stone walls, and old beams supported by wooden pillars. There are two bars, front and back. The back bar is used mainly by families, although children are allowed in the front one if they are having a meal. The front bar is the more attractive. It is slightly marred by having a gas fire set in its old stone fireplace, but this does not detract too much from the appeal of the place. The restaurant was closed for refurbishment when we visited, but from the little we saw, it is in keeping with the rest of the pub.

The place is said to be haunted by three ghosts, all apparently friendly, although their sex and history is not known!

Food:

There is a range of bar snacks, including burgers, ploughman's lunches, sandwiches and vegetarian dishes. When the restaurant is open, there is a separate restaurant menu. A speciality is their roast Sunday dinner.

Local Interest:

See previous entry.

Walks:

See previous entry.

North Bovey

40. The Ring of Bells

Map Reference:	741839
Open:	11.00-3.00, 6.00-11.00
Type:	Free house
On Draught:	Pedigree, Dartmoor Best, Wadworth 6X, Burton Ale, Whitbread Trophy, Guinness, Castlemaine Lager, Carlsberg Export, Strongbow Cider
Children:	Yes
Dogs:	Yes
Food:	Midday and evening (bar menu only at midday)
Letter Box Stamp:	Yes
Parking:	In the village
Accommodation:	5 rooms, including a family room, all with en suite bathrooms
Facilities:	Restaurant. Beer garden. Darts, pool. Outdoor swimming pool for residents.

Description:
A rambling old pub set back from the road. It was originally built in 1248 as a lodging house for the masons building the local church. It is a lovely old place, full of atmosphere, with two bars and a lounge at one end, and a restaurant at the other. The full range of food is served in both the bars and the restaurant because the landlord "doesn't want it to become known as a posh 'restaurant' type pub".

The large bar is fairly basic, with a stone floor, a pool table and a darts board. Next door to it is a smaller, cosier bar with attractive bench seats and stools, while the lounge has tables and chairs and a large fireplace containing a small enclosed fire. The attractive restaurant is completely separate from the rest of the pub. The beer garden is in the courtyard at the front.

Kitty Jay is said to have committed suicide in the pub. She is famous as the supposed occupant of Jay's Grave, a well-known landmark near Cripdon Down and not far from Hound Tor, a servant who was made pregnant by her employer's son and committed suicide out of shame. It is said that there are always fresh flowers on her grave, no matter what the time of year. Certainly the previous landlady believed the place was haunted, either by Kitty Jay or someone else. She refused to sleep on the premises under any circumstances. Haunted or not, the pub is now very popular with walkers.

Food:
Both the bar menu and the full menu (available evenings only) have a wide range of dishes, including vegetarian and children's meals. There are also daily specials, including such things as pheasant. The food is excellent.

Local Interest:
North Bovey is a little village of very pretty white-painted cottages

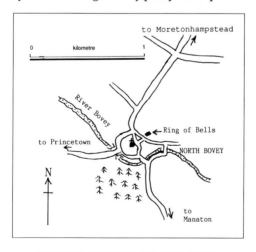

THE RING OF BELLS, NORTH BOVEY

south-west of Moretonhampstead. There is pony trekking nearby, and golf at the Manor House Hotel just north-west of the village.

Walks:
North Bovey is a marvellous centre for walking, with paths in every direction. There is a very pleasant circular walk to Moretonhampstead and back (which can be extended to take in Butterdon Down) to the north. Lustleigh Cleave, another delightful circuit, lies to the south-east, Manaton and the Becka Valley to the south and Easdon Tor, Coombe Down and the Two Moors Way to the south-west. To complete the circle round the compass, there are paths and lanes all the way to Chagford to the north-west.

Peter Tavy

41. The Peter Tavy Inn

Map Reference:	512777
Open:	11.30-2.30 (11.30-3.00 on Saturdays), 6.30-11.00
Type:	Free house
On Draught:	A succession of real ales which change all the time - about 5 or 6 are on tap at any one time; also Tetley, Guinness, Lowenbrau Lager, Warsteiner Lager, Skol Lager, Inch's Stonehouse Cider
Children:	In the snug, beer garden and restaurant (if eating)
Dogs:	In the bar, on a lead
Food:	Midday and evening (restaurant evenings only)
Letter Box Stamp:	Pub stamp and various "specials"
Parking:	Yes. Ask about overnight parking.
Accommodation:	No
Facilities:	Restaurant. Beer garden. Darts.

Description:

A beautiful fifteenth-century pub with small, comfortable rooms, full of traditional charm and character. There are three rooms: the bar, the snug and the restaurant. The biggest of the three is the bar, which has a stone floor and an enclosed fire. The snug also has a stone floor, and is a cosy, friendly little room. The restaurant is also fairly small, with more modern decor, but still in character with the pub.

There is a delightful story about a vicar of the church up the lane, who sent his churchwarden down to the pub on Sundays to make sure that no one was drinking during his service. The warden, however, had divided loyalties, as he was related to the publican. So as he walked over from the church, he would keep his eyes on the ground, looking neither left nor right, saying "I'm coming, Cousin Tom, I'm coming, Cousin Tom" over and over. The drinkers would all hide when they heard him coming, so he could truthfully report back to the vicar that he had seen no one drinking during the service!

Walkers are very welcome here, and of course, with the stone floors, there is no problem about boots, wet waterproofs and other paraphernalia.

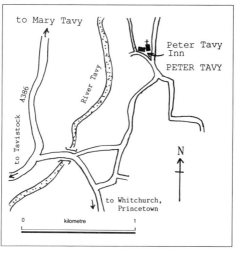

THE PETER TAVY INN, PETER TAVY

Food:
There is a wide range of bar snacks and daily specials on the board, including main meals and vegetarian dishes. There is a full à la carte menu in the restaurant, but only in the evenings.

Local Interest:
Peter Tavy is a small, attractive village between Tavistock and Mary Tavy, with a lovely church. The main attractions of the area are the beauty of the countryside and the variety of the walking.

Walks:
The walking here is as varied as you will find anywhere. From the pub you can walk north to reach the beautifully wooded Tavy Valley, with lanes and farm paths taking you even further north to Horndon. To the east, lanes and paths take you to Smeardon Down, White Tor and as far as you care to go on the open moor. And to the south-east paths and lanes soon lead you to Cox Tor, Great Staple Tor and a further choice of destinations. Moreover, there are several circular routes that combine a variety of terrains. Beware on the open moor, however. This is a military range, so check firing times before you go too far.

Postbridge

41a. The East Dart Hotel

Map Reference:	649790
Open:	11.00-11.00
Type:	Free house
On Draught:	John Smith's, Courage Best, Directors, Fosters Lager, Carlsberg Lager, Kronenbourg Lager, Guinness
Children:	Yes
Dogs:	Yes
Food:	Midday and evening

The Tavistock Inn, Poundsgate

The Warren House Inn, near Postbridge

The Plume of Feathers, Princetown
The White Thorn, Shaugh Prior

Letter Box Stamp: Yes

Parking: Small car park. Public car park just down the road.

Accommodation: 13 rooms, 5 with en suite bathrooms

Facilities: Dining room. Walkers' room. Pool, darts. Stabling and grazing.

Description:

The East Dart was a favourite haunt of walkers for many years, but it closed towards the end of 1991. It re-opened while this book was in production, so, thanks to some quick work on the part of the publisher, we have been able to include it.

It is an eighteenth-century inn, originally a temperance hotel. There is a large bar, the front part of which has a parquet floor, while the back section, half-partitioned off, is carpeted. There is a large stone fireplace and chimney breast with an enclosed fire, oak beams and a frieze of hunting scenes around the walls. The bar is furnished with settles, stools, chairs and tables, and there is a light, airy dining

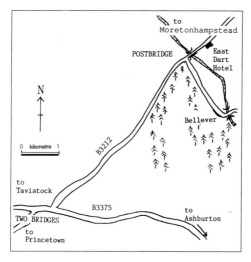

THE EAST DART HOTEL, POSTBRIDGE

room, which is open to non-residents.

One of the outhouses at the back is being converted into a games room and a special walkers' room where you will be able to spread your gear out, dry off and relax with your food or drink without worrying about how the non-walkers might react. This is not to say that walkers are not wanted in the main bar - they are very welcome everywhere in the hotel. But it is nice to have somewhere dedicated specially to walkers.

This is a pleasant pub, very popular with walkers and riders both because of its position near to one of the wildest parts of the moor and because of its friendly atmosphere.

Food:
The food is basic but good. There are separate bar and dining room menus, with a good choice of dishes, as well as daily specials.

Local Interest:
Postbridge, on the B3212 between Two Bridges and Moretonhampstead is noted for its ancient clapper bridge, probably the most photographed bridge on Dartmoor. It is a popular place for holidaymakers and family outings, as there are some pleasant strolls along the East Dart River. Powder Mills, with its pottery open to the public, is nearby.

Walks:
There are walks on both sides of the river, with a path leading east towards Pizwell and Soussons Warren and several going south and south-east to Bellever Forest and beyond. Across the road from the pub you can walk on to the open moor and choose your own route. But beware, this stretch of moorland is part of a military range. So check on firing times before venturing too far.

nr Postbridge

42. The Warren House Inn

Map Reference:	809674
Open:	10.30-2.30, 5.30-11.00 (all day in summer)
Type:	Free house
On Draught:	Flowers Original, Flowers IPA, Wadworth 6X, Bishop's Tipple, Murphy's Stout, Taunton Cider
Children:	Yes
Dogs:	Yes
Food:	Midday and evening (bar snacks only at midday)
Letter Box Stamp:	Pub stamp and seasonal stamps
Parking:	On the roadside
Accommodation:	No
Facilities:	Darts, pool table, skittles on request. Video games. Pub sweatshirts and postcards available.

Description:
An isolated pub on the B3212 between Postbridge and Moretonhampstead. The original inn stood on the other side of the road, but it was moved to its present site in 1845, since when the fire has never been allowed to go out - tradition has it that this is to keep the Devil away. There are in fact two fires, one at each end. It is very much a traditional pub (originally frequented by the tin miners from the workings round about), with stone floor, beams and old wooden benches and settles.

There is an amusing story about the Warren House. One bitter winter a traveller called asking for accommodation. In his room, he found a large chest. Unable to contain his curiosity, he opened it to see what was inside. To his horror, he found a corpse! However, the landlord put his mind at rest. "Don't worry," he said. "It's only

Father." The old man had died a few weeks earlier, and his body had been salted to preserve it until the weather broke and it could be carried across the moor for burial.

Modern visitors get a somewhat less traumatic reception and walkers are particularly welcome - no problem with muddy boots and dripping waterproofs on the stone floor. The pub is popular with the more serious walkers, and there are usually a few kindred spirits in the bar discussing routes and weather conditions.

Food:
Bar snacks are available midday and evening, but main meals and steaks are only served in the evening. Devonshire cream teas are also on offer.

Local Interest:
High and isolated, the pub is surrounded by open moorland. Grimspound (an impressive prehistoric settlement) is $1^1/2$ miles (2.5km) to the east.

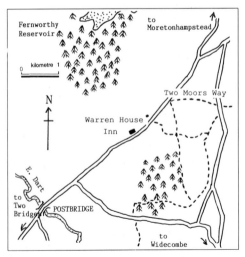

THE WARREN HOUSE INN, NR POSTBRIDGE

Walks:
Since the pub is in open moorland, the choice of walks is almost endless. There are several interesting and beautiful routes taking in Grimspound, from a short stroll up to the enclosure itself to a 16-mile (27km) circuit which also includes Hamel Down, Corndon Tor, Birch Tor and Shapley Common, with many variations in between. The Two Moors Way passes nearby.

Poundsgate

43. The Tavistock Inn

Map Reference:	705721
Open:	11.00-3.00, 6.00-11.00 (all day in summer)
Type:	Courage house
On Draught:	Webster's, Courage Best, Beamish Stout, Kronenbourg Lager, Fosters Lager, Dry Blackthorn Cider
Children:	With the landlord's permission
Dogs:	On a lead
Food:	Midday and evening
Letter Box Stamp:	No
Parking:	Car park across the road. No overnight parking, but ask for suggestions.
Accommodation:	No
Facilities:	Beer garden. Darts. Payphone in the car park. Quite a walk to the toilets, and it can be a bit breezy in winter!

Description:
Well over 700 years old, this lovely old pub retains its traditional charm and friendly atmosphere. It is very much a farmers' local, but visitors are given a warm welcome. It is renowned for its floral displays, and its garden has won a number of awards. There is one

smallish bar, beautifully beamed and with a concrete floor (so no need to worry about messy boots). There are large fires in winter, and in summer you can sit in the beautiful garden at the back or watch the world go by from the benches at the front.

Legend has it that the Devil called here for a drink in 1638, on his way to claim a soul in Widecombe. The landlady was delighted when this strange traveller paid in gold coins, but became suspicious when she heard the beer sizzle as it went down his throat. Her suspicions were confirmed when the traveller left and the gold coins turned to dried leaves.

Another story tells of a regular customer known as "the Snail", who was always being abused by one of his fellow drinkers. Then one night, for no apparent reason, he was polite to him. He even bade him good night, something he had never done before. That very night the Snail died! The locals helped to pay for his burial as he only had seven pence to his name when he died.

Food:
There is an extensive menu available in the bar, including vegetarian

THE TAVISTOCK INN, POUNDSGATE

dishes, all freshly prepared. The speciality is poached fish, and the chips are said to be excellent.

Local Interest:
Poundsgate is a tiny hamlet on the road from Ashburton to Dartmeet. At Dartmeet, where the two branches of the River Dart, the East and West Dart, converge, there are very popular picnic areas by the river. There is good canoeing on the Dart.

Walks:
There are some delightful walks, both long and short, along lanes and paths towards Spitchwick and the River Dart to the east and south, and there are tors to explore to the west. If you follow Dr Blackall's Drive between Mel Tor and Aish Tor, you will be rewarded with some stunning views over the Dart Gorge. The Two Moors Way passes about 3 miles (5km) to the east.

Princetown

44. The Devil's Elbow

Map Reference:	591785
Open:	11.00-11.00
Type:	Free house
On Draught:	Whitbread Poacher, Flowers IPA, Winter Royal, Boddingtons, Guinness, Heineken Lager, Dry Blackthorn Cider
Children:	Yes
Dogs:	Yes
Food:	Midday and evening
Letter Box Stamp:	A selection of about 10 stamps
Parking:	Yes. Ask about overnight parking.
Accommodation:	7 rooms
Facilities:	Beer garden. Children's room. Pool, skittles, darts, euchre, chess.

Description:

This nineteenth-century inn, formerly the Railway Hotel, comprises a row of converted cottages. Although it has a somewhat rundown appearance, it is quite a pleasant pub, with two bars and a small snug. The front bar is panelled, with an open fire, and the cosy little snug lounge leads off it. Since there is no bar in the snug, children eating with their parents usually sit there.

The other bar, called the Stable Bar, is at the back of the pub and is opened when needed. It has bare stone walls and a pleasant, comfortable atmosphere. It leads directly on to the children's room, so it is useful for parents, who can sit there with their children next door. It is also used as a function room. The beer garden, which has direct access to the car park, needs some attention. It is, of course, popular with letter-boxers because of the variety of stamps available.

Two of the bedrooms are said to be haunted by an old woman, although no one knows who she might be.

Food:

There is a good range of bar snacks, as well as hot meals and a children's menu. The speciality is locally caught trout - not farmed but caught by a local fisherman.

Local Interest:

Princetown is not a very attractive village, but the surrounding moorland is impressive. The village's main claim to fame is as the home of Dartmoor Prison, whose sombre bulk can be seen to the north.

Walks:

The walking round Princetown is all on open moorland - and fairly wild moorland at that. You can therefore walk almost anywhere in the area, but care is needed in winter or in bad weather. There are military firing ranges to the north, so you should check on firing times before venturing in that direction. To the south-east, beyond South Hessary Tor and Whiteworks lies Foxtor Mires, a notorious area of bog which has been the death of more than one unwary traveller.

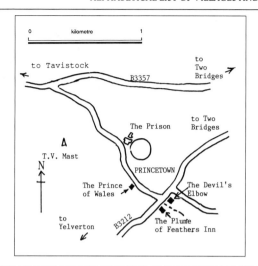

THE DEVIL'S ELBOW, THE PLUME OF FEATHERS AND
THE PRINCE OF WALES, PRINCETOWN

45. The Plume of Feathers Inn

Map Reference:	591735
Open:	11.00-11.00
Type:	Free house
On Draught:	Tinners, Hicks, Bass, Guinness, Tennents Extra, Tennents Pilsner, Carlsberg Lager, Dry Blackthorn Cider
Children:	Yes
Dogs:	On a lead and under control - there are sheep in the fields behind the pub
Food:	Midday and evening
Letter Box Stamp:	No
Parking:	Yes. Ask about overnight parking.
Accommodation:	5 rooms (1 double, 4 family); alpine bunkhouse with 20 bunk beds in 2 dormitories, cooking

	facilities and day room; camping area for 75 tents, with shower and toilet block.
Facilities:	Beer garden, picnic area and children's adventure play area. Family room. Function room. Darts. Skittle alley. Dance floor. TV, juke box.

Description:
Built in 1785, this inn is the oldest building in Princetown, and retains many of its original features - granite walls, slate floors, exposed beams etc. It is full of atmosphere, with copper bars and oil lamps. There is a public bar with a small bar but plenty of seating and an open fire, and a beamed lounge, also with an open fire, decorated with an interesting collection of ships' shields. The tables are made from slabs of slate on iron frames.

The pub has a friendly, welcoming atmosphere, and walkers are well catered for, with a wide range of different kinds of accommodation to choose from. You will usually find a few kindred spirits warming themselves by the fire in winter or sunning themselves in the garden in summer.

Food:
There is an extensive menu, ranging from bar snacks (toasted sandwiches, jacket potatoes, pasties etc.) to main meals and vegetarian dishes. All the food is freshly prepared.

Local Interest:
See previous entry.

Walks:
See previous entry.

46. The Prince of Wales

Map Reference:	589786
Open:	11.00-3.00, 6.30-11.00

Type:	Free house
On Draught:	Bass, Boddingtons, Wadworth 6X, Old Bodger (in winter), Whitbread Best, Heineken Lager, Stella Artois Lager, Bulmers Cider, Gaymers Olde English Cyder, Scrumpy Jack Cider
Children:	In the pool room
Dogs:	Yes
Food:	Midday and evening
Letter Box Stamp:	4 stamps
Parking:	Yes. Ask about overnight parking.
Accommodation:	No
Facilities:	Restaurant. Darts, pool, euchre, dominoes, pinball machine, fruit machine, juke box.

Description:
Built in 1854, this is a somewhat surprising pub. The rather unprepossessing exterior hides a very pleasant U-shaped bar with bare stone walls, a low beamed ceiling and two large open fires. (In fact there are three fireplaces, but one isn't used.) Furnished with high-backed chairs at the bar and tables and chairs elsewhere, there is a lot of atmosphere and a traditional "local" feel. The restaurant leads off the bar. It is a cosy room, also with stone walls, and very nicely decorated and furnished.

The pub is said to be haunted by the ghost of a former landlord who shot himself.

Food:
The pub offers a wide range of bar snacks as well as an à la carte restaurant menu.

Local Interest:
See previous entry.

Walks:
See previous entry.

Sandy Park

47. The Sandy Park Inn

Map Reference:	712896
Open:	11.00-3.00, 5.00-11.00
Type:	Free house
On Draught:	Flowers IPA, Flowers Original, Boddingtons, Brakspear, Pedigree, Murphy's Stout, Heineken, Dry Blackthorn Cider
Children:	In the snug
Dogs:	No
Food:	Midday and evening
Letter Box Stamp:	No
Parking:	On the forecourt and the road
Accommodation:	3 rooms, 1 with en suite bathroom
Facilities:	Darts. A few benches outside. T-shirts and sweatshirts available from the bar.

Description:
This sixteenth-century inn is very much a local pub, but visitors are given a friendly welcome. There is a cosy public bar and snug. The bar has a stone floor, scrubbed pine tables and a low-beamed ceiling, and oozes atmosphere. It is a traditional local bar, and one gets the impression that little has changed over the centuries. The snug is carpeted and has a rather more impersonal fee to it.

It is to the public bar that most walkers gravitate, partly because of the atmosphere and partly because there are no problems with muddy boots and dripping waterproofs on the stone floor. There is a blazing open fire in a cast-iron fireplace in the winter, and the landlord has no objection to people hanging wet socks in front of it!

Food:
There is not a very wide choice of food, but what there is is good. It

The Sandy Park Inn, Sandy Park

ranges from ploughman's lunches to duck with orange, and the menu changes from time to time.

Local Interest:
Sandy Park is just a small collection of houses (it hardly even warrants being called a hamlet) on the A382 between Moretonhampstead and Okehampton. It is only a few hundred yards from the River Teign.

Walks:
The main attraction for walkers in the area is the River Teign. The Two Moors Way goes along the river bank just south of Sandy Park, and it is possible to follow the river all the way to Steps Bridge, near Dunsford, in the east and to Leigh Bridge, just beyond Chagford, to the west. From Leigh Bridge you can cut across to the open moor via Teigncombe and Gidleigh Common or follow the Two Moors Way southwards to Fernworthy Reservoir and beyond.

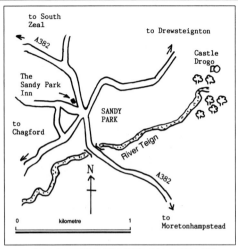

THE SANDY PARK INN, SANDY PARK

Scorriton

48. The Tradesman's Arms

Map Reference:	704685
Open:	11.30-2.30, 6.30-11.00 (summer) 7.00-11.00 (winter) (closed on Mondays in winter)
Type:	Free house
On Draught:	Wadworth 6X, Dartmoor Best, Ansells, Guinness, Carlsberg Export, Castlemaine Lager
Children:	In the family room
Dogs:	No
Food:	Midday and evening
Letter Box Stamp:	No
Parking:	Yes. Ask about overnight parking.

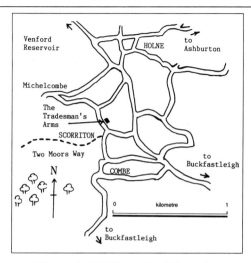

THE TRADEMAN'S ARMS, SCORRITON

Accommodation: No

Facilities: Family room with games. Beer garden. Darts.

Description:
Built about 300 years ago to serve the tin miners from the moor (the "trade" from which it probably derives its name), this pub offers a pleasant atmosphere and a friendly welcome, and is frequented by the local farmers. It is also popular with walkers. There are two bars. The main one is not particularly elegant, with plastic-covered bench seats and stools, but it does have the advantage of an open fire in winter, where one can dry out. The snug bar, on the other hand, is a delightful little room, nicely furnished, cosy and attractive, but it has no fire. So you pays your money and takes your choice. The family room has extensive views of the surrounding countryside.

Food:
There is a range of bar snacks, including sandwiches, basket meals and ploughman's lunches, as well as daily specials.

The Trademan's Arms, Scorriton

Local Interest:
Scorriton is a small, unspoilt village between Buckfastleigh and
Holne, the centre of a farming area. There is pony trekking nearby.

Walks:
There are some delightful short rambles along field and woodland
paths and lanes to Scae Wood and Chalk Ford, and longer walks up
on to the moor to the west via Scorriton Down and Buckfastleigh
Moor, with magnificent views as you go. Alternatively, you can
head north-east past Holne to Venford Reservoir. The Two Moors
Way passes through the village.

Shaugh Prior

49. The White Thorn

Map Reference:	632539
Open:	11.00-2.30, 6.00-11.00
Type:	Courage house

On Draught:	Royal Oak, Courage Best, Directors, John Smith's, Beamish Stout, Fosters Lager, Kronenbourg Lager, Dry Blackthorn Cider
Children:	Ask
Dogs:	Yes
Food:	Midday and evening
Letter Box Stamp:	Pub stamp and seasonal stamps
Parking:	Yes. Ask about overnight parking.
Accommodation:	No
Facilities:	Darts, games. Good toilets. Restaurant. Local home-made leather goods on sale over the bar.

Description:

A large pub with a single, fairly large bar. Plenty of seating, spacious and comfortable. The oak beams, horse-brasses, open fire and friendly landlord and staff give a cosy, welcoming atmosphere. There is a large beer garden at the back, also with plenty of seating, and with direct access to the car park. The pub is frequented by a

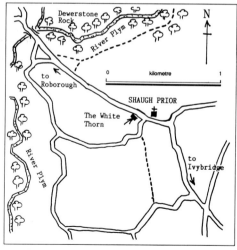

THE WHITE THORN, SHAUGH PRIOR

horse called Flash whose favourite tipple is stout!

Walkers are welcomed, but since the bar is nicely carpeted, a little consideration wouldn't come amiss if it is wet and muddy outside. The pub is well used by the walking fraternity and by outdoor enthusiasts generally. It is particularly popular with letter-boxers.

A legend associated with the pub tells of a man on his way home after an evening's drinking. On the way he met old Dewer (the Devil), returning from his evening's hunting. Emboldened by the drink, the man called up to him: "Good hunting tonight?"

"Excellent," replied old Dewer. "And since you ask, here's a present for you." And with that, he threw down a bag and rode off. Imagine the man's horror, when he got home and opened the bag, to find it contained the body of his daughter!

Food:
Very good, ranging from snacks to three-course meals. A speciality is the lamb roasts held outside from time to time in the summer.

Local Interest:
Shaugh Prior is on the south-west edge of Dartmoor. A short walk from the village is Shaugh Bridge across the River Plym, at the point where the Meavy and the Plym meet. It is a popular site for picnics and family days out and also for rock climbing.

Walking:
There is a bracing walk up to the Dewerstone Rock (where old Dewer, the Devil, was said to throw his victims over the edge), with fine views of the moor to the north and Plymouth Sound to the south, and excellent rocks for the climbing enthusiast. There are also several pleasant woodland and riverside walks through National Trust property.

South Brent

50. The Anchor

Map Reference:	698601
Open:	11.00-3.30, 6.00-11.00 (all day Fridays and Saturdays)
Type:	Free house
On Draught:	Bass, Flowers IPA, Worthington Best, Murphy's Stout, Guinness, Castlemaine Lager, Carlsberg Lager, Copperhead Cider, Luscombe's Farm Cider
Children:	Yes
Dogs:	Yes
Food:	Midday and evening
Letter Box Stamp:	Yes
Parking:	There is a free car park at the old station, about 100 yards up the road, or park on the street
Accommodation:	No
Facilities:	Function room. Pool, darts, euchre, cards etc.

Description:
This old posting inn was badly damaged by fire in 1990, but it has been very well restored, and is now probably closer to the original in appearance and atmosphere than it was before the fire. There are two bars, both half-carpeted, with a lot of timber beams and panelling, beautiful stone walls and an open fire in the lounge bar. The pub has a very traditional atmosphere about it which is difficult to define but which makes it a comfortable place to relax.

It is popular with walkers, indeed the local walking fraternity congregate here.

Food:
A range of bar snacks is usually offered, although the kitchen was

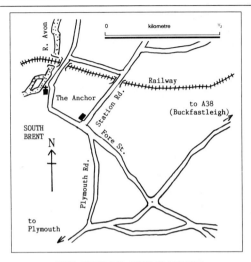

THE ANCHOR, SOUTH BRENT

still out of action as a result of the fire at the time of our visit, so there was no food available.

Local Interest:
South Brent is a fairly large village on the southern edge of Dartmoor. The village itself does not have very much to offer (although the church is interesting), but there is fishing on the River Avon.

Walks:
Most of the best walks are to the north of the village (although with a fair amount of road walking, you can also reach an extensive network of paths to the west). There is a lovely gentle stroll, lined with rhododendrons and beech trees, along the banks of the Avon to Lydia Bridge (³/₄ mile/1km). This can be extended further up the valley to Shipley Bridge (2 miles/3.5km) or further still to the Avon Dam (4 miles/6.5km). You can also venture out of the valley on to the moors to the west, and if you go one way via the valley and the other via the moors, you have a delightfully varied walk. The local walkers sometimes go even further, picking up the Abbot's Way at

the Avon Dam and going all the way to Princetown for a drink at the Plume of Feathers before returning home again, a round trip of some 27 miles (44km) - a long way to go for a drink!

South Zeal

51. The Oxenham Arms

Map Reference:	651935
Open:	11.00-2.30, 6.00-11.00
Type:	Free house
On Draught:	Tinners, Bass, Guinness, Carlsberg Lager, Stella Artois Lager
Children:	In the family room and garden
Dogs:	Yes
Food:	Midday and evening
Letter Box Stamp:	No
Parking:	Small forecourt. More parking in the road.
Accommodation:	10 rooms, all with en suite bathrooms
Facilities:	Family lounge. Large garden at the rear. Dining room. Residents' lounge.

Description:
A beautiful old granite inn, believed to date back to the twelfth century. It was built by lay monks and later became the Dower House of the Burgoyne family, through whose heiress it passed to the Oxenham family - hence its name. The Oxenhams, whose line has now died out, suffered from visitations by an apparition of a white bird. If it was seen near a member of the family it indicated that he or she was about to die.

The inn is one of the most picturesque in the area, with old beams, stone walls and leaded windows, and is a delightful place to stay or stop for a drink or a meal. There is a cosy L-shaped bar, partly panelled, with a beautiful granite fireplace and a small family lounge. Set in the wall of this lounge is a monolith believed to date back 5,000 years. The dining room is also full of character. There is a large garden laid to grass at the back with extensive views across the moors to Cawsand Beacon. The residents' lounge is tastefully furnished with leather armchairs and a beautiful old writing desk, and the stairs and landing leading to the bedrooms contain period furniture, a feature which gives the whole place a homely atmosphere.

The Oxenham Arms is celebrated in literature. It features in Eden Philpott's *The Beacon* and in Baring Gould's *John Herring*. The legend of the white bird is told in Charles Kingsley's classic, *Westward Ho!*.

Considerate walkers are welcomed - indeed there is a heater in the hall over which wet clothing can be dried in winter.

Food:
There is a range of food available, ranging from bar snacks to three-course meals.

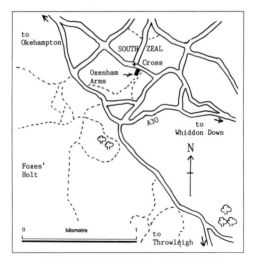

THE OXENHAM ARMS, SOUTH ZEAL

Local Interest:
South Zeal is a picturesque old single-street village on the northern edge of the moor, which does not appear to have changed much over the centuries. The street is dominated by a very small and charming old church which seems to have been built in the middle of the road.

The Eggesford and Mid-Devon Foxhounds meet in the forecourt of the inn. There is fishing in local reservoirs and in the River Taw, and riding facilities are available nearby.

Walks:
There is a range of good walks in the area, from short strolls to long hikes. The village is dominated by Cawsand Beacon (marked on OS maps as Cosdon Beacon), about 2 miles (3km) away. There is also a very interesting circular walk to Little Hound Tor and back (6 miles/9.5km), taking in the stone row known as The Graveyard and the Whit Moor stone circle. This is open moorland, so there are almost limitless walking opportunities, but beware: it is one of the wildest parts of Dartmoor and great care is needed, particularly in bad weather. Moreover, this part of the moor forms part of the Okehampton Artillery Range, so if you are planning to go far you should check on firing times.

Sparkwell

52. The Treby Arms

Map Reference:	581579
Open:	11.00-3.00, 6.30-11.00 (flexible opening during summer)
Type:	Free house
On Draught:	Bass, Ruddles Best, Webster's, Worthington Best, Tennents Pilsner, Tennents Extra, Tennents LA, Holsten Export, Carling Black Label Lager, Taunton Cider
Children:	Only if eating

Dogs:	No
Food:	Midday and evening
Letter Box Stamp:	Yes
Parking:	Yes. Ask about overnight parking.
Accommodation:	No
Facilities:	Darts euchre, cribbage.

Description:

This delightful old pub dates back to 1750. It is a small, cosy place with just one bar and a few tables outside. The bar is in a semi-horseshoe shape, with a low-beamed ceiling and an open stove which is lit in winter. (The landlord keeps the letter box stamp in the stove, so if it can't be found, you will know that he's set light to it!)

The pub contains a collection of old bottles, jugs and brass mugs, and there is an interesting array of stained glass shields above the bar. The floor is half tiled, half carpeted. It is a pub with a lot of character and there is a warm welcome from both the landlord and the locals.

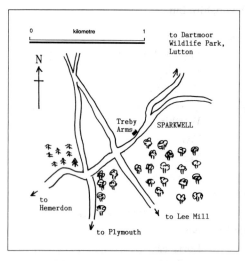

THE TREBY ARMS, SPARKWELL

Food:
There is a range of bar snacks and main meals including steaks.

Local Interest:
Sparkwell is a picturesque village a few miles outside the south-western boundary of the National Park. Not far from the village is the Dartmoor Wildlife Park, a very popular venue for holiday-makers.

Walks:
Most of the walking from Sparkwell is to the north, but there are several routes to choose from in that direction. North-west lie the disused mines and workings of Hemerdon Ball and Crownhill Down, and north-east you can walk to Yondertown, Lutton and beyond to the National Park proper.

Sticklepath

53. The Devonshire Inn

Map Reference:	641940
Open:	11.00-3.00, 5.30-11.00 (all day Fridays and Saturdays)
Type:	Free house
On Draught:	Tinners, Winter Warmer, Hicks, Bass, Worthington Best, Guinness, Carlsberg Lager
Children:	Yes
Dogs:	Yes
Food:	Midday and evening
Letter Box Stamp:	Yes
Parking:	Car park across the road
Accommodation:	No
Facilities:	Darts, cards, cribbage, shove ha'penny, fruit machine.

Description:

This is a beautiful old sixteenth-century inn with three rooms. To the right as you come into the pub is the bar, a cosy little room, with magnificent Elizabethan fireplace and a linoleum floor, "specially for the walkers". Beyond that is a small snug, with its own fire, nicely carpeted and furnished with armchairs and an attractive inlaid table.

To the left of the entrance is what is called the pool room, another small room with its own fire. It is furnished with a large central table and chairs and there is an interesting collection of spears and guns.

The atmosphere is comfortable and friendly and walkers are particularly welcome - hence the linoleum floor!

Food:

Bar snacks are available and home-cooked ham is a speciality.

Local Interest:

Sticklepath is a pleasant little village just to the east of Okehampton, just outside the National Park boundary. The surrounding

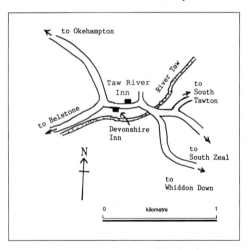

THE DEVONSHIRE INN AND THE TAW RIVER INN, STICKLEPATH

countryside is Tarka the Otter country and there is horse-riding nearby. There is a museum of water-power in the village.

Walks:
There is a lovely walk along the Taw River to Belstone, and beyond to Belstone Common, and to the south lies Cawsand Beacon (marked on the OS map as Cosdon Beacon), Little Hound Tor and the open moor. But beware: this is very wild country and care should be taken, especially in bad weather. If you are venturing some way, you will probably also be entering the military range, so check on firing times.

54. The Taw River Inn

Map Reference:	642941
Open:	12.00-3.00, 7.00-11.00
Type:	Free house
On Draught:	Ruddles County, Ruddles Best, Triple Crown, Webster's, Ushers Best, Guinness, Carlsberg Lager, Strongbow Cider
Children:	In the games room and garden
Dogs:	On a lead
Food:	Midday and evening
Letter Box Stamp:	Yes
Parking:	There is a large car park behind the pub. To find it you have to go down a lane to the side.
Accommodation:	4 rooms
Facilities:	Beer garden. Games room. Pool, darts, fruit machines. Live jazz every Monday.

Description:
This building dates back to the fourteenth century. It is a lovely old traditional thatched Devon longhouse and was originally the manor house of Sticklepath. There is a large bar divided by stone pillars, with low beams and a big open fire. The walls are attractively

123

papered. There is an interesting collection of ties and baseball caps over the bar.

There is also a pleasant games room, also with an open fire, and with a pool table and darts board, and a beer garden at the back, with direct access to the car park.

Food:
The menu ranges from bar snacks to a wide range of main meals.

Local Interest:
See previous entry.

Walks:
See previous entry.

Two Bridges

55. The Two Bridges Hotel

Map Reference:	609750
Open:	11.00-3.30 (summer) - 11.00-3.00 (winter), 6.00-11.00
Type:	Free house
On Draught:	Prisoner's Poison (their own ale), Courage Best, John Smith's Beamish Stout, Hofmeister Lager, Kronenbourg Lager, Carlton LA, Autumn Gold Cider
Children:	Yes
Dogs:	Yes
Food:	Midday and evening
Letter Box Stamp:	Yes
Parking:	Large car park. Overnight parking across the road.
Accommodation:	24 rooms, 20 with en suite bathrooms

Facilities: Dining room. Beer garden with direct access to the car park. Non-smoking lounge.

Description:
This two-star hotel is a favourite with walkers. Built in the eighteenth century, it has two elegant lounges furnished with armchairs and tables, one as you enter the hotel and the other (the non-smoking lounge) to the right.

The L-shaped bar has its own separate entrance, and it is here that walkers tend to gather. It is panelled, with pleasant little booths in one arm of the L, and is furnished with settles and chairs. There is a blazing open fire in winter, in a large stone fireplace with an unusual panelled chimney-breast and an interesting collection of padlocks. The walls are decorated with old photographs and prints.

The pleasant dining room opens on to both the bar and the lounge, and there is a large beer garden across the car park by the river. In summer, after a long walk (and most walks in this area tend to be long), there is nothing better than to sit in the garden, contemplating the river with a drink in your hand.

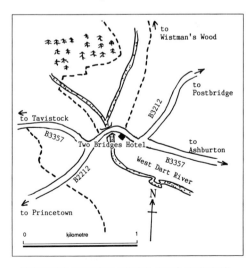

THE TWO BRIDGES HOTEL, TWO BRIDGES

Food:
There is a wide range of snacks and hot meals available, with daily "specials", including vegetarian dishes. The dining room is not open at midday in winter, but the full range of meals is available in the bar, so that is not a problem. A speciality is the Friday and Saturday carvery.

Local Interest:
Two Bridges is a place on the map to the east of Princetown, not a town or village, and apart from the two bridges which give it its name, the hotel is all there is to it. Wistman's Wood, a fascinating area of stunted oaks which form the last remnants of the ancient forests that covered this area, lies to the north.

Walks:
Two Bridges is at the crossroads of the moor, both literally and figuratively. Four roads converge here, and so do any number of walks. You can take a short stroll up to Wistman's Wood and back or choose from a wide variety of longer walks. North to Higher White Tor and beyond, south to Whiteworks and the dangers of Foxtor Mires, north-west towards Mary Tavy, north-east to Bellever Tor - the choices are almost endless. Just beware if you are heading towards the north: this is a military range, so check on firing times. It is also wild country, so go prepared for the terrain and the weather.

Walkhampton

56. The Walkhampton Inn

Map Reference:	533697
Open:	11.00-3.00, 6.00-11.00
Type:	Courage house
On Draught:	Directors, Courage Best, John Smith's, Guinness, Fosters Lager, Kronenbourg Lager, Red Rock Cider, Taunton Cider

Children:	In the garden and dining room
Dogs:	In the garden
Food:	Midday and evening
Letter Box Stamp:	4 new stamps each year
Parking:	Yes
Accommodation:	No
Facilities:	Beer garden with access to a children's play area. Darts, pool, euchre, dominoes.

Description:

A beautiful seventeenth-century inn full of charm and character - a typical traditional country pub. There are three cosy, comfortable, interconnected rooms, the end one of which serves as the dining room. The walls are of granite, with superb beams overhead, and a large collection of horse brasses (over 600) and hunting horns (there is a strong connection with the local hunt, which meets here). There is a 180-year-old oven which is still in use.

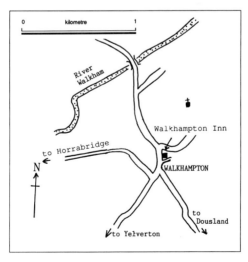

THE WALKHAMPTON INN, WALKHAMPTON

Food:
There is a range of bar food, with a wide and constantly changing selection of "specials" on the blackboard. They do excellent steak and kidney pies made from local meat.

Local Interest:
Walkhampton is an interesting old village with a beautiful Saxon church. It also boasts a working water-wheel, which drives the machinery for the local wheelwright, who still makes equipment for horse-drawn carriages, and whose workshop can be viewed from the road.

Walks:
Walkhampton marks the point where the Abbot's Way leaves "civilisation" and heads across the open moor all the way to Buckfastleigh. There are some delightful walks north to the River Walkham, from which the village takes its name, and north-east across Walkhampton Common to Princetown. Two miles (3.5km) to the south-east lies Burrator Reservoir, a popular picnic spot, with some beautiful walks through the forest there.

Whitchurch

57. The Whitchurch Inn

Map Reference:	493727
Open:	11.00-3.00, 6.00-11.00 (all day Saturdays)
Type:	Free house
On Draught:	Bass, Toby, Worthington Best, Guinness, Tennents Extra, Dry Blackthorn Cider
Children:	Ask
Dogs:	On a lead
Food:	Midday and evening
Letter Box Stamp:	No

Parking:	In the road (please park carefully)
Accommodation:	No
Facilities:	Function room. Darts, shove ha'penny.

Description:
This delightful old thirteenth-century inn was built by monks as a church house, and is right beside the church. It is a small, cosy pub, with beautiful old oak beams and an open fire at one end of the bar. At the other end is a seating area with tables and chairs. The function room is called the Tithe Room, and an interesting feature is the tithe hole, through which the locals paid their tithes to the church.

Food:
There is a selection of bar snacks and main meals, and daily specials on the board. A speciality is their Sunday lunch, for which it is necessary to book in advance.

Local Interest:
Whitchurch is a delightful village just outside Tavistock, between

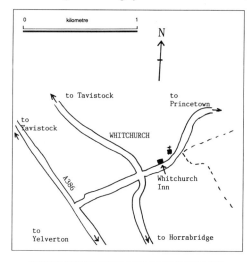

THE WHITCHURCH INN, WHITCHURCH

the A386 and the National Park boundary. The church, which is just beside the pub is particularly interesting and attractive.

Walks:
There are two paths leading off from almost outside the pub, one leading south-east to Boyton and on towards Horrabridge, and the other going east to Middle and on to Downhouse, from where lanes and further paths lead you on to Moortown, Pew Tor and Sampford Spiney. It is mainly farmland here, rather than typical moorland walking, but very pleasant, nevertheless.

Widecombe in the Moor

58. The Old Inn

Map Reference:	717767
Open:	11.00-3.00, 6.00-11.00
Type:	Free house
On Draught:	Widecombe Wallop (their own real ale), Ushers Best, Webster's, Ruddles County, Guinness, Carlsberg Lager, Fosters Lager, Holsten Pils
Children:	Yes
Dogs:	On a lead
Food:	Midday and evening
Letter Box Stamp:	No
Parking:	Yes. Ask about overnight parking.
Accommodation:	No, but they would be happy to advise you on where to find accommodation locally
Facilities:	Darts and pub games (winter only).

Description:
Partly because of its undoubted charm and partly because of the old song *Widecombe Fair*, this small village has become a popular

The Old Inn, Widecombe in the Moor

destination for holiday-makers and coach parties. As a result, both the village and the pub tend to be rather crowded in the summer.

Despite being a bit commercialised, this fourteenth-century inn is nevertheless a friendly and enjoyable place to stop for a drink or a meal. There is one bar, divided into a lower and an upper area. Wet and muddy walkers would probably do better to stick to the lower area, which is where people involved in outdoor pursuits tend to congregate anyway, and they prefer wet gear to be left outside. The lower area is warm and cosy, with low lighting, but it can become rather crowded in summer.

The inn is haunted by a ghost called Harry. He has been seen in mid-afternoon, walking from the kitchen to a room with no other exit. He then disappears. There is also the sobbing child, who has been heard but not seen. The sobbing sounds emanate from an upstairs room, but when the door is opened, the crying stops and there is no one there.

Food:
There is a good range of bar snacks and main meals, including daily specials.

Local Interest:
Widecombe is a pleasant if rather commercialised village. The church is a magnificent building, much larger than one would expect in a community of this size, with a very high tower which dominates the landscape. It has often been called the Cathedral of the Moor. The Church House is owned by the National Trust. Widecombe Fair is still held each year, on the second Tuesday in September.

Walks:
Widecombe is a good centre for walks of all kinds. There are some pleasant short walks in and around the village itself, while for the more adventurous there is Hamel Down to the west and a number of tors (Honeybag Tor, Chinkwell Tor, Top Tor and further on Haytor) to the east. The Two Moors Way passes just west of the village.

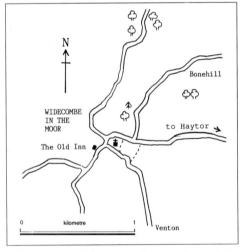

THE OLD INN, WIDECOMBE IN THE MOOR

Wonson

59. The Northmore Arms

Map Reference:	674897
Open:	All day
Type:	Free house
On Draught:	Whitbread Best, Flowers IPA, Ash Vine, Adnams Broadside, Murphy's Stout, Carlsberg Lager, Stella Artois Lager, Dry Blackthorn Cider
Children:	Yes
Dogs:	Yes
Food:	Midday and evening
Letter Box Stamp:	No
Parking:	Small car park, otherwise in the lane
Accommodation:	3 rooms, all with en suite bathrooms, 2 caravans, free camping in the field behind the pub
Facilities:	Beer garden. Darts.

Description:

This is a charming little pub, oozing atmosphere. It is about 400 years old, with the massive bare stone walls, small windows and large fireplaces that one associates with that period. It consists of two small interlinked rooms, each with its own open fire. It is very much a local pub, and there is a constant exchange of banter between the landlord and his regulars, into which the visitor is soon drawn.

It is named after the Northmore family who owned Wonson Manor, across the road, until one of the family lost his whole estate on the turn of a card in 1710. It was originally just a cider house, but became a pub in 1902 when the Rector of Throwleigh, the nearest village, closed the pub there. Since then, the villagers have had to make the ³/₄-mile (1.25km) journey up to Wonson for a drink.

The pub is very popular with walkers, and also with pony trekkers. It lies on the route from North Devon to Dartmouth which was used in the past by sailors changing ships, and is said to be haunted by the ghost of an old bearded sailor - presumably one who didn't make it to his new ship!

Food:
There is a fairly basic (but good) menu of bar snacks and a selection of interesting daily "specials".

Local Interest:
Wonson is a small hamlet not far from the attractive little village of Throwleigh. There is nothing of special interest locally - just beautiful countryside and good walking!

Walks:
Most of the walking to the north and east of Wonson is along lanes, with just the odd path to provide variety. To the south, however,

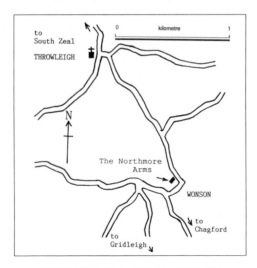

THE NORTHMORE ARMS, WONSON

you can follow lanes and paths to Gidleigh, and from there cross Gidleigh Park and join the Two Moors Way. And to the west lies the open moor. This is one of the wildest parts of the moor, so take care if you are walking in this direction, especially in bad weather. This is also where the artillery ranges are, so check on firing times before venturing out.

Yelverton

60. The Rock Inn

Map Reference:	522678
Open:	11.00-2.30, 6.00-11.00 (all day Saturdays, holidays and in summer)
Type:	Free house
On Draught:	Boddingtons, Bass, Bass IPA, Hicks, Pompey Royal, Worthington Best, Guinness, Carling Black Label Lager, Stella Artois Lager, Tennents Pilsner, Tennents Extra, Tennents LA
Children:	In the family room
Dogs:	Yes, except in the lounge
Food:	Midday and evening
Letter Box Stamp:	No
Parking:	Yes. Ask about overnight parking.
Accommodation:	No
Facilities:	Beer garden, fenced garden for children. Family room. Pool, darts, euchre, cribbage.

Description:
This is an old coaching inn dating from the seventeenth century, although it has been added to over the years, resulting in a rather strange conglomeration of styles. It has been in the same family since 1874.

The Rock Inn, Yelverton

There are three bars and a family room. The public bar has the original stone walls, and is carpeted, with upholstered bench seats. It has an enclosed fire and a very cosy atmosphere, and this is the bar that walkers tend to use. The lounge bar is similar to the public bar, although it is a bit smaller and the walls are papered. It also has an

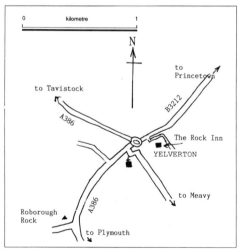

THE ROCK INN, YELVERTON

enclosed fire. You are asked not to use this bar with muddy boots.

The games room bar is not quite as plush as the other two. It is a large, comfortable room, and as its name suggests, this is where the games are. Walkers are, of course, welcome in this room as well. The family room is also pleasant, with a beautiful painting by a local artist. Off the family room is a small room which is used as a video room.

Food:

There is a range of bar snacks and meals, including vegetarian dishes, plus a range of daily specials on the board.

Local Interest:

Yelverton is a somewhat nondescript village on the A386 between Plymouth and Tavistock. Roborough Rock, on the outskirts of the village, is popular with families, and Burrator Reservoir is not far away to the east.

Walks:

There is not much walking from Yelverton itself, although there is a delightful path from Roborough Rock southwards along the valley of the Meavy to Clearbrook. Indeed, you can do a circuit by following the valley to Clearbrook and coming back via Chub Tor. Apart from that, you would need to drive a little way to find any good walking.

*   *   *

ALPHABETICAL LIST OF PUB NAMES
BY NUMBER

✳   ✳   ✳

CICERONE GUIDES

Cicerone publish a wide range of reliable guides to walking and climbing abroad

FRANCE
TOUR OF MONT BLANC
CHAMONIX MONT BLANC - A Walking Guide
TOUR OF THE OISANS: GR54
WALKING THE FRENCH ALPS: GR5
THE CORSICAN HIGH LEVEL ROUTE: GR20
THE WAY OF ST JAMES: GR65
THE PYRENEAN TRAIL: GR10
THE RLS (Stevenson) TRAIL
TOUR OF THE QUEYRAS
ROCK CLIMBS IN THE VERDON
WALKS IN VOLCANO COUNTRY (Auvergne)
WALKING THE FRENCH GORGES (Provence)
FRENCH ROCK

FRANCE / SPAIN
WALKS AND CLIMBS IN THE PYRENEES
ROCK CLIMBS IN THE PYRENEES

SPAIN
WALKS & CLIMBS IN THE PICOS DE EUROPA
WALKING IN MALLORCA
BIRDWATCHING IN MALLORCA
COSTA BLANCA CLIMBS
ANDALUSIAN ROCK CLIMBS

FRANCE / SWITZERLAND
THE JURA - Walking the High Route and
 Winter Ski Traverses
CHAMONIX TO ZERMATT The Walker's Haute
Route

SWITZERLAND
WALKING IN THE BERNESE ALPS
WALKS IN THE ENGADINE
WALKING IN TICINO
THE VALAIS - A Walking Guide
THE ALPINE PASS ROUTE

GERMANY / AUSTRIA
THE KALKALPEN TRAVERSE
KLETTERSTEIG - Scrambles
WALKING IN THE BLACK FOREST
MOUNTAIN WALKING IN AUSTRIA
WALKING IN THE SALZKAMMERGUT
KING LUDWIG WAY
HUT-TO-HUT IN THE STUBAI ALPS

ITALY
ALTA VIA - High Level Walkis in the Dolomites
VIA FERRATA - Scrambles in the Dolomites
ITALIAN ROCK - Rock Climbs in Northern Italy
CLASSIC CLIMBS IN THE DOLOMITES
WALKING IN THE DOLOMITES

MEDITERRANEAN COUNTRIES
THE MOUNTAINS OF GREECE
CRETE: Off the beaten track
Treks & Climbs in the mountains of RHUM &
PETRA, JORDAN
THE ATLAS MOUNTAINS
WALKS & CLIMBS IN THE ALA DAG (Turkey)

OTHER COUNTRIES
ADVENTURE TREKS - W. N. AMERICA
ADVENTURE TREKS - NEPAL
CLASSIC TRAMPS IN NEW ZEALAND

GENERAL OUTDOOR BOOKS
THE HILL WALKERS MANUAL
FIRST AID FOR HILLWALKERS
MOUNTAIN WEATHER
MOUNTAINEERING LITERATURE
THE ADVENTURE ALTERNATIVE
MODERN ALPINE CLIMBING
ROPE TECHNIQIUES IN MOUNTAINEERING
MODERN SNOW & ICE TECHNIQUES
LIMESTONE -100 BEST CLIMBS IN BRITAIN

CANOEING
SNOWDONIA WILD WATER, SEA & SURF
WILDWATER CANOEING
CANOEIST'S GUIDE TO THE NORTH EAST

CARTOON BOOKS
ON FOOT & FINGER
ON MORE FEET & FINGERS
LAUGHS ALONG THE PENNINE WAY
BLACKNOSE THE PIRATE

*Also a full range of guidebooks
to walking, scrambling, ice-climbing,
rock climbing, and other adventurous
pursuits in Britain and abroad*

*Other guides are constantly being added to the Cicerone List.
Available from bookshops, outdoor equipment shops or direct (send for price list)
from CICERONE, 2 POLICE SQUARE, MILNTHORPE, CUMBRIA, LA7 7PY*

CICERONE GUIDES

Cicerone publish a wide range of reliable guides to walking and climbing in Britain, and other general interest books.

LAKE DISTRICT - General Books
A DREAM OF EDEN
LAKELAND VILLAGES
LAKELAND TOWNS
REFLECTIONS ON THE LAKES
OUR CUMBRIA
THE HIGH FELLS OF LAKELAND
CONISTON COPPER A History
LAKELAND - A taste to remember (Recipes)
THE LOST RESORT?
CHRONICLES OF MILNTHORPE
LOST LANCASHIRE
THE PRIORY OF CARTMEL

LAKE DISTRICT - Guide Books
CASTLES IN CUMBRIA
THE CUMBRIA CYCLE WAY
WESTMORLAND HERITAGE WALK
IN SEARCH OF WESTMORLAND
CONISTON COPPER MINES Field Guide
SCRAMBLES IN THE LAKE DISTRICT
MORE SCRAMBLES IN THE LAKE DISTRICT
WINTER CLIMBS IN THE LAKE DISTRICT
WALKS IN SILVERDALE/ARNSIDE
BIRDS OF MORECAMBE BAY
THE EDEN WAY

NORTHERN ENGLAND (outside the Lakes
THE YORKSHIRE DALES A walker's guide
WALKING IN THE SOUTH PENNINES
WALKING IN THE NORTH PENNINES
LAUGHS ALONG THE PENNINE WAY
WALKS IN THE YORKSHIRE DALES (3 VOL)
WALKS IN LANCASHIRE WITCH COUNTRY
WALKS TO YORKSHIRE WATERFALLS
MORE WALKS TO YORKSHIRE WATERFALLS
NORTH YORK MOORS Walks
THE CLEVELAND WAY & MISSING LINK
DOUGLAS VALLEY WAY
THE RIBBLE WAY
WALKS ON THE WEST PENNINE MOORS
WALKING NORTHERN RAILWAYS EAST
WALKING NORTHERN RAILWAYS WEST
HERITAGE TRAILS IN NW ENGLAND
BIRDWATCHING ON MERSEYSIDE
THE LANCASTER CANAL
ROCK CLIMBS LANCASHIRE & NW
THE ISLE OF MAN COASTAL PATH
CANOEISTS GUIDE TO THE NORTH EAST
THE NORTHERN COAST-TO-COAST

DERBYSHIRE & EAST MIDLANDS
WHITE PEAK WALKS - 2 Vols
HIGH PEAK WALKS
WHITE PEAK WAY

KINDER LOG
THE VIKING WAY
THE DEVIL'S MILL (Novel)
WHISTLING CLOUGH (Novel)
WALES & WEST MIDLANDS
THE RIDGES OF SNOWDONIA
HILLWALKING IN SNOWDONIA
HILL WALKING IN WALES (2 Vols)
ASCENT OF SNOWDON
WELSH WINTER CLIMBS
SNOWDONIA WHITE WATER SEA & SURF
SCRAMBLES IN SNOWDONIA
SARN HELEN Walking Roman Road
ROCK CLIMBS IN WEST MIDLANDS
THE SHROPSHIRE HILLS A Walker's Guide
HEREFORD & THE WYE VALLEY A Walker's Guide
THE WYE VALLEY WALK

SOUTH & SOUTH WEST ENGLAND
THE SOUTHERN-COAST-TO-COAST
WALKS IN KENT
THE KENNET & AVON WALK
THE WEALDWAY & VANGUARD WAY
SOUTH DOWNS WAY & DOWNS LINK
COTSWOLD WAY
WALKING ON DARTMOOR
WALKERS GUIDE TO DARTMOOR PUBS
EXMOOR & THE QUANTOCKS
SOUTH WEST WAY - 2 Vol

SCOTLAND
THE BORDER COUNTRY - WALKERS GUIDE
SCRAMBLES IN LOCHABER
SCRAMBLES IN SKYE
THE ISLAND OF RHUM
CAIRNGORMS WINTER CLIMBS
THE CAIRNGORM GLENS (Mountainbike Guide)
THE ATHOLL GLENS (Mountainbike Guide)
WINTER CLIMBS BEN NEVIS & GLENCOE
SCOTTISH RAILWAY WALKS
TORRIDON A Walker's Guide
SKI TOURING IN SCOTLAND

THE MOUNTAINS OF ENGLAND & WALES
VOL 1 WALES
VOL 2 ENGLAND
THE MOUNTAINS OF IRELAND
THE ALTERNATIVE PENNINE WAY
THE RELATIVE HILLS OF BRITAIN
LIMESTONE - 100 BEST CLIMBS

Also a full range of EUROPEAN guide-books - walking, long distance trails, scrambling, ice-climbing, rock climbing.

Other guides are constantly being added to the Cicerone List.
Available from bookshops, outdoor equipment shops or direct (send s.a.e. for price list) from
CICERONE, 2 POLICE SQUARE, MILNTHORPE, CUMBRIA, LA7 7PY

PRINTED BY
CARNMOR PRINT & DESIGN, LONDON ROAD, PRESTON